RECC

I

Hotel prices in New York are, by most standards, high. However, almost all hotels offer weekend packages with reductions of 20% to 50%. These may include free museum passes, theatre tickets and brunch or dinner. In addition, special rates, at a discount of about 20–25%, are usually available during slow times of the year such as in summer. It's always wise to reserve your room in advance. Many hotels offer a toll-free ("1-800" numbers are free of charge) and fax service.

Most hotels have either double or twin beds in all rooms, whether for single or double occupancy. The incremental charge for double occupancy is only 10–20% of single occupancy. The prices below are based on cost per mid-week night, double occupancy of an average room, and do not include taxes (see p. 100) and tips. Unless otherwise stated, all rooms have bathrooms en suite with a tub or shower and toilet. Most hotels have individual climate controls, cable colour TVs and direct-dial phones. Breakfast is rarely included.

▮ below $100 ▮▮ $100–200 ▮▮▮ above $200

Chatwal Inn on 48th St. ▮

234 W. 48th St., NY 10036 (Broadway and Eighth Ave.). Tel. 246-8800/ 1-800-826-4667, fax 974-3922.

400 rooms. Handsome Theater District hotel. Striking lobby with sky-lit atrium and a waterfall.

Doral Court ▮▮

130 E. 39th St., NY 10016 (at Lexington Ave.).
Tel. 685-1100/1-800-624-0607, fax 889-0287.

199 rooms. A pretty hotel in a residential area south of Grand Central Station. Spacious rooms.

Gramercy Park Hotel ▮▮
2 Lexington Ave., NY 10010 (at E. 21st St.). Tel. 475-4320/1-800-221-4083, fax 505-0535.
500 rooms. Quiet friendly and quaint old-world residence.

The Helmsley Middletowne Hotel ▮▮
148 E. 48th St., NY 10017 (Lexington and Third aves.). Tel. 755-3000/1-800-221-4982, fax 832-0261.
192 rooms. Quiet and very comfortable lodgings near the UN.

The Helmsley Palace ▮▮▮
455 Madison Ave., NY 10022 (E. 50th and 51st sts.). Tel. 888-7000/1-800-221-4982, fax 888-1074.
773 rooms. Located behind St. Patrick's Cathedral, the modern 55-storey Palace incorporates the restored 19th-century Villard Houses.

Herald Square Hotel ▮
19 W. 31st St., NY 10001 (at Fifth Ave.). Tel. 279-4017/1-800-727-1888, fax 643-9208. Some rooms with shared bathrooms.
130 rooms. This restored 19th-century home of *Life* magazine is located three blocks south of the Empire State Building.

Holiday Inn Crowne Plaza ▮▮
1605 Broadway, NY 10019 (W. 48th and 49th sts.). Tel. 977-4000/1-800-465-4329, fax 333-7393.
770 rooms. This black-glass structure towers 46 storeys above Times Square. Marble bathrooms and health club with large indoor pool.

Hotel Beverly ▮▮
125 E. 50th St., NY 10022 (at Lexington Ave.). Tel. 753-2700/1-800-223-0945.
220 rooms. A family-owned establishment in busy East Side location.

Hotel Esplanade ▮▮
305 West End Ave., NY 10023 (at W. 74th St.). Tel. 874-5000/1-800-367-1763, fax 496-0367.
200 rooms. This landmark building near Lincoln Center has spacious rooms, some overlooking the river. Reasonable rates. Health club.

Hotel Iroquois ▮
49 W. 44th St., NY 10036 (Fifth and Sixth aves.). Tel. 840-3080/1-800-332-7220, fax 827-0464.
125 rooms. Pleasantly renovated and centrally located hotel. Suites with fully equipped kitchenettes.

Hotel Macklowe ▮▮▮

145 W. 44th St., NY 10036 (Sixth Ave. and Broadway). Tel. 768-4400/ 1-800-622-5569, fax 768-0847.

638 rooms. A 52-storey contemporary Art-Deco tower off Times Square. Guest rooms with high-tech electronics and excellent health club.

Hotel Wales ▮▮

1295 Madison Ave., NY 10028 (at E. 92nd St.).
Tel. 876-6000/1-800-223-0888, fax 860-7000.

92 rooms. One of the city's oldest hotels, the elegantly restored Wales is situated in a residential neighbourhood on the Upper East Side.

Hôtel Plaza Athénée ▮▮▮

37 E. 64th St., NY 10021 (Park and Madison aves.). Tel. 734-9100/ 1-800-447-8800, fax 772-0958.

156 rooms. A European-style hotel on the Upper East Side boasting French period furnishings, hand-painted murals and excellent cuisine.

Malibu Studios Hotel ▮

2688 Broadway, NY 10025 (W. 103rd and 104th sts.). Tel. 222-2954, fax 678-6842. Some units with private bathrooms.

150 studios. Clean budget lodgings on the Upper West Side.

The Mark ▮▮▮

25 E. 77th St., NY 10021 (at Madison Ave.).
Tel. 744-4300/1-800-843-6275, fax 744-2749.

182 rooms. This stylish and comfortable Upper East Side establishment offers Italian neoclassical suites, Piranesi prints and afternoon tea.

The Mayflower Hotel ▮▮

15 Central Park West, NY 10023 (W. 61st and 62nd sts.). Tel. 265-0060/ 1-800-223-4164, fax 265-5098.

377 rooms. An old-world hotel with rooms overlooking Central Park.

Paramount Hotel ▮▮

235 W. 46th St., NY 10036 (Broadway and Eighth Ave.). Tel. 764-5500/ 1-800-225-7474, fax 354-5237.

610 rooms. A stylish Theater District hotel with health club, cinema, video library and children's playroom.

Pickwick Arms Hotel ▮

250 E. 51st St., NY 10022 (Second and Third aves.). Tel. 355-0300/ 1-800-742-5945, fax 755-5029. Some rooms with shared bathrooms.

400 rooms. Attractive budget hotel in residential area.

Portland Square Hotel ▮

132 W. 47th St., NY 10036 (Sixth and Seventh aves.). Tel. 382-0600, fax 382-0684. Some rooms with shared bathrooms.
110 rooms. Nicely restored 1904 Theater District hotel.

Ramada Hotel ▮▮

790 Eighth Ave., NY 10024 (W. 48th and 49th sts.). Tel. 581-7000/ 1-800-228-2828, fax 974-0291.
366 rooms. This 15-storey hostelry features clean rooms and an open-air rooftop swimming pool.

Salisbury Hotel ▮▮

123 W. 57th St., NY 10019 (Sixth and Seventh aves.). Tel. 246-1300/ 1-800-223-0680, fax 977-7752.
320 rooms. Two blocks south of Central Park, the Salisbury offers pleasant and spacious rooms.

United Nations Plaza Hotel ▮▮▮

1 U.N. Plaza, NY 10017 (First Ave. and E. 44th St.). Tel. 355-3400/ 1-800-228-9000, fax 702-5051.
428 rooms. In this sculptured glass skyscraper opposite the UN, guest rooms begin on the 28th floor. Fitness centre, indoor swimming pool and tennis court.

The Waldorf-Astoria ▮▮▮

301 Park Ave., NY 10022 (E. 49th and 50th sts.). Tel. 355-3000/ 1-800-445-8667, fax 758-9209.
1,408 rooms. Situated just behind Grand Central Station, New York's most "royal" hotel includes an elaborate fitness centre, theatre and tour desks, shops, bars and several restaurants.

Washington Square Hotel ▮

103 Waverly Pl., NY 10011 (Washington Sq. and Sixth Ave.). Tel. 777-9515/1-800-222-0418, fax 979-8373. Some rooms with shared bathrooms.
200 rooms. Attractively restored 1902 hotel in the heart of Greenwich Village.

Wyndham Hotel ▮▮

42 W. 58th St., NY 10019 (Fifth and Sixth aves.). Tel. 753-3500.
185 rooms. The Wyndham, close to Central Park, is a charming, privately owned and affordable hotel with spacious, old-fashioned rooms.

RECOMMENDED RESTAURANTS

Restaurants are categorized by the approximate cost of a three-course à la carte dinner for one, excluding drinks, tax and tips. Many establishments serve reasonably priced "prix fixe" and pre-theatre dinners and weekend brunches. Reservations are recommended.

▮ below $15 ▮▮ $15–35 ▮▮▮ above $35

Akbar ▮▮

475 Park Ave. (E. 57th and 58th sts.). Tel. 838-1717.

Indian. Authentic North Indian cuisine in a sky-lit room. Good tandoori chicken and chicken ginger kebab. Vegetarian specialities. Also at 256 E. 49th St. (tel. 755-9100).

American Festival Café ▮▮

Rockefeller Center, 20 W. 50th St. (Fifth and Sixth aves.). Tel. 246-6699.

American. Overlooking the famous skating rink, the Café takes over the Lower Plaza in summer with pink umbrellas, geraniums and a fountain lit in pastel colours. Specialities: cold poached salmon, Maryland crab cakes, prime rib.

Aquavit ▮▮▮

13 W. 54th St. (Fifth and Sixth aves.). Tel. 307-7311.

Scandinavian. A sensational two-tiered atrium (the upper floor café is less expensive than the restaurant downstairs). Marinated salmon, smoked Arctic venison, *smorgasbord* platters and herb-flavoured aquavits. Closed Saturday lunch time and Sunday.

Benny's Burritos ▮

113 Greenwich Ave. (at Jane St.). Tel. 727-0584.

Californian-Mexican *burritos* (steamed flour *tortillas*) with fresh fillings (lamb, turkey, vegetarian) are washed down with margaritas in rowdy Village bar.

La Bonne Soupe
48 W. 55th St. (Fifth and Sixth aves.). Tel. 586-7650.
Hearty soups served with salad, bread, dessert and drink in atmospheric French midtown bistro. Also egg, fish and meat dishes.

Bouley
165 Duane St. (Hudson and Greenwich sts.). Tel. 608-3852.
French. Superb Provençal cuisine served in a pretty restaurant in TriBeCA. The menu includes lobster, grilled or in red-wine sauce, sautéed scallops, braised or roasted pigeon and fruity soufflés. Closed Saturday lunch time and Sunday.

Broadway Diner
1726 Broadway (at W. 55th St.). Tel. 765-0909.
A white-tiled '50s-style diner dishing out huge portions.

Brother's Bar-B-Que
228 W. Houston St. (near Varick St.). Tel. 727-2775.
Barbecued chicken, ribs and beef brisket in a SoHo diner booming with soul music.

Cabana Carioca
123 W. 45th St. (Sixth and Seventh aves.). Tel. 581-8088.
Brazilian. A popular Theater District dining spot serving huge portions of *mariscada* seafood stew and *feijoada,* a tangy stew of black beans, meat and sausage.

Carnegie Delicatessen & Restaurant
854 Seventh Ave. (at W. 55th St.). Tel. 757-2245.
Legendary deli serving pastrami (seasoned smoked beef) and corned-beef sandwiches.

Condon's
117 E. 15th St. (Union Sq. East and Irving Pl.). Tel. 254-0960.
American. An intimate grotto for good bistro food (Maryland crab cakes) and live jazz. Garden.

Elephant & Castle
68 Greenwich Ave. (near Seventh Ave.). Tel. 243-1400.
Village café known for its juicy burgers, fluffy omelettes and good salads and desserts. Also in SoHo at 183 Prince St. (tel. 260-3600).

The Four Seasons

99 E. 52nd St. (Park and Lexington aves.). Tel. 754-9494.

Continental/international. Housed in the landmark Seagram Building, the Four Seasons is rated a culinary institution. Try the Grill Room for lunch—crab cakes, grilled fish and meat—and the Pool Room for dinner—ragout of lobster, crisp farmhouse duck, game in season. Grill Room closed Sunday, Pool Room Saturday lunch time and Sunday.

Golden Unicorn

18 E. Broadway (at Catherine St.). Tel. 941-0911.

Chinese. A lively Hong Kong-style restaurant, some say Chinatown's best. Try a plate of *dim sum* (filled dumplings and other food in bite-size portions).

Gotham Bar & Grill

12 E. 12th St. (Fifth Ave. and University Pl.). Tel. 620-4020.

American. A vast, strikingly designed Greenwich Village establishment famous for its *haute cuisine*: seafood salads, subtle fish dishes (tuna, bass), smoked duck, herb-and-mustard basted rack of lamb. Closed Saturday and Sunday lunch time.

Les Halles

411 Park Ave. South (E. 28th and 29th sts.). Tel. 679-4111.

French. A genuine Parisian bistro specializing in *charcuterie* platters, cassoulets, steak tartar.

John's Pizza

278 Bleecker St. (at Seventh Ave.). Tel. 243-1680.

In Greenwich Village, probably the best pizzas in New York.

The Manhattan Ocean Club

57 W. 58th St. (Fifth and Sixth aves.). Tel. 371-7777.

American. An excellent seafood restaurant, the two-tiered Club, adorned with Picasso plates and paintings, specializes in baked oysters and clams, grilled swordfish, salmon steak and spicy crab cakes. Closed Saturday and Sunday lunch time.

Oyster Bar & Restaurant

Grand Central Terminal, lower level (E. 42nd St. at Vanderbilt Ave.). Tel. 490-6650.

American. A vast dining hall offers juicy oysters (sold by the piece), fresh fish, shellfish stews and chowders (hearty seafood soups). Closed Saturday and Sunday.

Pasta Pot ▮

160 Eighth Ave. (at W. 18th St.). Tel. 633-9800.

Inviting Italian eatery in Chelsea, featuring some 20 different kinds of pasta.

The Rainbow Room ▮▮▮

30 Rockefeller Plaza (W. 49th and 50th sts.). Tel. 632-5000.

Continental. On the 65th floor of the RCA Building, the city's most fashionable supper club serves up dishes like oysters Rockefeller, lobster thermidor and tournedos Rossini. Dinner only. Closed Monday.

Serendipity 3 ▮

225 E. 60th St. (Second and Third aves.). Tel. 838-3531.

Toy shop-restaurant dishes out foot-long hot dogs, burgers, tiny pizzas and hot fudge sundaes.

Sevilla ▮▮

62 Charles St. (Seventh Ave. and W. 4th St.). Tel. 929-3189.

Spanish. In the Village, this rustic room filled with Spanish music features fabulous *paellas* and fruity sangria.

Shinwa ▮▮

645 Fifth Ave. (at E. 51st St.). Tel. 644-7400.

Japanese. Enjoy *sushi* by an indoor waterfall and reflecting pool, or, in winter, order *zosui,* a porridge of rice, scallops and spinach. Closed Sunday.

Soho Kitchen and Bar ▮▮

103 Greene St. (Spring and Prince sts.). Tel. 925-1866.

American. Pizzas, pastas, grilled fish, salads, burgers and over 100 varieties of wine by the glass in casual SoHo eatery decorated with art pieces.

Symphony Café ▮▮

950 Eighth Ave. (at W. 56th St.). Tel. 397-9595.

American. Handsome and casual café with fine cuisine: home-made pasta, salmon steaks, roasted duckling.

Windows on the World ▮▮▮

1 World Trade Center (Vesey and Liberty sts.). Tel. 938-1111.

International. The view, the wine list and the weekend brunch are the main attractions of this 107th-floor downtown establishment. Seafood specialities.

BERLITZ®

NEW YORK

By the staff of Berlitz Guides

Printed in Switzerland by Weber S.A., Bienne.

13th Printing
1992/1993 Edition

HOW TO USE THIS GUIDE

- All the practical information, hints and tips that you will need before and during the trip start on page 99.
- For general background, see the sections New York and the New Yorkers, page 7, and A Brief History, page 13.
- All the sights to see are described between pages 21 and 78. Our own choice of sights most highly recommended is pinpointed by the Berlitz traveller symbol.
- For hotel and restaurant recommendations, see the yellow pages in the centre of the guide.
- Shopping, entertainment and sports are recounted from pages 81 to 89. There is a special section on page 90 to help you entertain your children, while information on restaurants and cuisine is to be found between pages 93 and 98.
- If there's anything you can't find, look in the index, pages 127–128.

Although we have made every effort to ensure the accuracy of all the information in this book, changes occur incessantly. We cannot therefore take responsibility for any facts, prices, addresses and circumstances in general that are constantly subject to alteration.

Text: Martine Lamunière
Staff Editor: Kathryn-Jane Müller-Griffiths
Layout: Doris Haldemann
Photography: Erling Mandelmann; pp. 74–75 PRISMA/West Light; cover Jean Mohr
Cartography: Falk-Verlag, Hamburg

We would like to thank Ken Bernstein, Barbara Ender, Sandra P. Griffiths and Anne-Karin Ratna for their invaluable help in the preparation of this guide.

CONTENTS

New York and the New Yorkers		7
A Brief History		13
What to See	Midtown	21
	Downtown	37
	Uptown	52
	Museums	62
	Excursions	73
What to Do	Shopping	81
	Entertainment	84
	Sports	87
For Children		90
Eating Out		93
Blueprint for a Perfect Trip		99
Index		127

Hotel and Restaurant Recommendations	between 64 and 65

Maps	New York City	22
	Greenwich Village	49
	Subway	122
	Midtown Manhattan	124
	Wall Street	126

For further information on New York, in a handy pocket size, see The New York City Address Book, *also published by Berlitz. Packed with hundreds of essential addresses of hotels, restaurants, shops, art galleries, museums, and lots more, the Address Book will provide the perfect complement to this travel guide.*

FRAMES
THE RUSSIAN TASTE

NEW YORK AND THE NEW YORKERS

Okay, New York is crowded, dirty, noisy and impolite! But it is undeniably one of the world's most exciting cities. Other Americans often fear and dislike New York. With a typical shrug, New Yorkers dismiss this as provincial jealousy. Fire sirens may wail all night while steam billows hellishly from the manholes, walls and fences may be defaced by graffiti, and people may move faster than taxis. So what? New York is the place where it's all happening!

This is the Big Apple: Wall Street and its dollars, Rockefeller Center with its multinational corporations, Madison Avenue manipulating the media, the United Nations with its diplomacy. Dynamic? And how!

Put your skates on and get down to the Met.

Look at the nervous knot of pedestrians waiting for the traffic light to change: a Wall Street tycoon, dark-suited; a chic black model with her portfolio; an Orthodox Jew straight out of the Old Testament; a Latin American—more Latin than American but in a rush like everybody else; to say nothing of the multitudes of Chinese, Italians, Irish, Greeks, Eastern Europeans...

Even the language of New York—locals tend to say "Noo Yawk"—is not quite American. Spoken in a mumbled rush, it's a tough brand of English with the exaggeration of Madison Avenue, the sarcasm of the street-wise kid and a few words of Yiddish and Italian as punctuation.

New York is in many respects a "refugee camp". The immigrants who didn't want to be blended into the American melting pot stayed in the area. They settled in New York to keep their own values and whatever they could preserve of their native culture. Variety and tolerance are the bywords here. You can do and say whatever you like and nobody will bat an eyelid.

Of course you'll want to see the skyscrapers. Chicago's may be more beautiful (and in one case taller) but those in Manhattan, the island heart of New York, will impress you with their overwhelming abundance. A veritable forest of glass and steel! Then, for a change of pace, explore some residential neighbourhoods. Greenwich Village will enchant you with its tree-lined streets (yes, real trees!) and tidy brownstone

Get the lowdown on Manhattan's high-rises from Brooklyn Heights.

houses, reminiscent of London or Amsterdam. On the Upper West Side you may smile at the huge Victorian apartment buildings topped with Moorish arches, Babylonian turrets or Gothic spires. In New York you need eyes in the top of your head.

First-time visitors are often nervous about New York because of its size, relentless pace and reputation for violence. Crime certainly is a problem, with its roots in poverty. You don't have to venture far from the glittering centre to see desolate streets with abandoned and gutted buildings. New Yorkers don't try to hide the problem. They've simply had to learn to live with it.

Just relax and prepare for all the excitement of a great port, a

NEW YORK IN FIGURES

New York is bigger, taller and more impressive than anywhere else. If you want proof, here are a few figures:

—The five boroughs (Manhattan, Brooklyn, Queens, the Bronx and Staten Island) have a total population of 8 million. With the surrounding suburbs, this figure rises to 12 million and, if the outlying satellite cities are included, the total attains a phenomenal 16 million inhabitants.

—New York City covers an area of 300 square miles. It has 6,400 miles of streets and 18 miles of beaches. There are 1,100 parks, squares and playgrounds with a total area of 37,000 acres; 100 museums and 400 galleries; more than 30 department stores; 400 theatres; about 100 skyscrapers; 3,500 churches; 15,000 restaurants; 100,000 first-class hotel rooms and 12,000 taxis.

—About 4 million people ride the subway every day. Some 2½ million catch a bus. The number of shops is well up in the thousands. Roughly 17 million people visit New York each year, 2½ million of them from overseas.

In New York there are more Italians than in Venice, more Irish than in Dublin and more Jews than in any other city in the world.

world capital of fashion, finance and culture. Business and art coexist effortlessly here—from a pharaoh's tomb to pop art, New York money has endowed dozens of memorable museums. It's the creative-arts centre of the U.S., perhaps the world. Broadway invented the musical and crowds queue in Central Park to see free Shakespeare.

But do save some time for shopping, too. From discount emporia to that esoteric item you've always been looking for, the choice is enormous. And don't miss this unique opportunity for a whirlwind gastronomic tour of the globe. Whether charcoal grilled or whipped up in a wok, you name it, New York's got it!

Admittedly everything about New York is excessive, including the climate: too hot in summer, too cold in winter. "You have to be a little crazy to live in New York", according to a subway poster, "crazy about shows, restaurants, theaters, shopping". New Yorkers, with their well-concealed hearts of gold, really do love their town. They hope you will, too.

St. Patrick's Gothic spires are now overshadowed by glittering glass.

LET US RAISE A STANDARD TO WHICH THE WISE
AND THE HONEST CAN REPAIR THE EVENT
IS IN THE HAND OF GOD WASHINGTON

A BRIEF HISTORY

When Giovanni da Verrazzano, a Florentine in the service of France, set foot on Staten Island, he hardly dreamed that the bay he had discovered would one day become the site of the most powerful city in the world. That was in 1524, just 32 years after Christopher Columbus's first voyage to America. Today a bridge bearing his name (but spelt with one "z") stretches elegantly across New York Bay.

Verrazzano was well received by the Manhattans, a local tribe of Indians who guided his ship to a safe landing. Although he wrote an enthusiastic report of his visit to the French king, François I, a century passed before any settlers actually came to live on the estuary.

Washington Arch—the gateway to the trendy, fashion-conscious world of Greenwich Village.

New Amsterdam

In 1609 an Englishman, Henry Hudson, was sent to look for a westward route to the Indies. He didn't find what he was after, but he sailed up the broad river (later named after him) and discovered the beautiful Hudson Valley. Returning to Holland with quantities of furs, fruit and tobacco, Hudson stirred up a great deal of interest. A group of merchants founded a company, which was to have a trading monopoly in the area. Then, in 1621, the Dutch West India Company was granted the charter to trade, plant colonies and defend its outposts in North and South America. The first settlers arrived under the company's auspices in 1624, ousting the French, who were there only hours before them. The following spring they built a small town on the southern end of Manhattan Island and called it New Amsterdam.

For 40 years the Dutch remained in possession of Manhattan, purchased from the Indians for the legendary sum of $24. Under the leadership of two governors, Peter Minuit and Peter Stuyvesant, the town took on a Dutch look, yet from the beginning it was the most cosmopolitan centre in the New World. The earliest immigrants included Walloons, Scandinavians, Germans, Englishmen, Spaniards and Portuguese Jews, not to mention black slaves from the Caribbean. In 1643 a priest counted 18 languages spoken in this town of 1,500 inhabitants. Other settlements had developed outside Manhattan in what is now the Bronx, in Brooklyn and in the Flushing area of Queens.

Life was by no means easy, though. In those days of poor communications, it was practically impossible to do anything without prior approval from the home country. Relations with the Indians were tense and the climate was harsh. What's more, the British—who held all the colonies around New York—were knocking at the door.

Unable or unwilling to put up a fight, the Dutch settlers surrendered to the Duke of York's troops on September 8, 1664. New Amsterdam was rechristened New York. The Dutch briefly retook the city in 1673 (renaming it New Orange) but, by the Treaty of Westminster of the following year, Manhattan and New Netherland became definitively English.

In the 18th century the town grew into a city of 25,000. Life became more comfortable. A city hall and several fine churches were built, and New York saw the foundation of King's College and the creation of its first newspaper. Many traders were able to make their fortunes. However, the people were increasingly irked by British control. New York, like the other colonies, was split between "loyalists" to the Crown and "patriots" who favoured independence. On June 27, 1775, half the town went to cheer Washington as he left to take command of the Revolutionary Army in Boston, while the other half were down at the harbour giving a rousing welcome to the English governor, who had just returned from London. Similarly, the New York delegates voted against an early version of the Declaration of Independence. But a few days later, when the final text had been drafted, they signed it.

Even in those days New Yorkers were a people apart from other Americans.

The New Republic

After a series of battles around New York, their last stronghold, the English finally gave up in 1783, recognizing the independence of the American colonies. Washington returned triumphantly to New York and bade farewell to his troops at Fraunces Tavern (see p. 38). He came back again on another auspicious occasion: to take the oath of office as the first president of the new United States on the balcony of Federal Hall (at that time New York was the national capital).

In the early 19th century New York was much richer culturally than any other American city. The political capital had moved to Philadelphia in 1790 but New York developed as the country's shipping and commercial centre. In 1800 the population was 60,000—twice what it had been ten years earlier. Already the city had problems that persist today: housing shortages, too few policemen and firemen, not enough water and inadequate public transportation facilities. Epidemics were frequent, sometimes forcing people to "escape" to Greenwich Village for the summer.

In 1811 the legislature decided that any further growth of New York must be regulated. A special commission submitted a revolutionary plan: all new streets should henceforth cross each other at right angles with avenues running north–south and streets east–west. The plan was immediately adopted, heralding the birth of Manhattan as we know it today.

Burgeoning Town

When the Erie Canal opened in 1825, New York became the ocean gateway for the Great Lakes region. Business flourished and shipyards abounded in this major port, but even so there was too little work for newcomers. Blacks, Irish and German immigrants lived on top of each other in crowded shanty towns. The Catholic Irish were resented, and religious conflicts erupted.

In December 1835, a terrible fire destroyed the heart of the business district, including all that remained from the Dutch era. But the city recovered with amazing speed. Old neighbourhoods were soon rebuilt, with the new, wealthy banks putting up the buildings that still stand in Wall Street. There was much construction uptown, too: in 1853 the Crystal Palace of the first American World's Fair went up, and five years later work started on Central Park and St. Patrick's Cathedral. In spite of the new prosperity, this was also a very turbulent period for New York. Between 1840 and 1860 the city's population rose from 300,000 to 800,000. Riots, demonstrations and street fights were not uncommon.

With the Civil War, the town's growth came to a temporary halt. New Yorkers were markedly unenthusiastic about the Union cause, and the draft law—providing for a $300 exemption fee—met with ferocious opposition from the foreign-born working class.

After the war the boom continued unabated to the end of the century. It gave rise to unprecedented corruption on a vast scale and to wild property speculation. Financiers Jay Gould and Jim Fisk cornered the gold market, ruining half of Wall Street on "Black Friday" in September 1869. Boss Tweed of the Tammany Hall political organization ran New York with his cohorts and managed to fleece the city of something like $200 million. Many great fortunes were made more or less honestly. The Vanderbilts constructed the railroads, and the Morgans, the banking tycoons, amassed fabulous art collections in an effort to gain acceptance among the "old families".

Mass Immigration

During the second half of the 19th century immigrants flooded in to New York in search of a new life. They came from Ireland and Germany, as always, but now also from Italy, Russia, Poland and Hungary. The first major wave of Jewish settlers arrived in the 1880s. Over 2 million newcomers landed in New York between 1885 and 1895, welcomed (after 1886) by the newly inaugurated Statue of Liberty (see p. 73). For the first time Congress imposed limits on immigration, banning the Chinese, the sick, madmen and anarchists.

Adequate housing for the constantly expanding working population was a great problem. A subsidized housing programme was launched but could hardly begin to deal with the situation. The new middle class moved to West Side neighbourhoods near Central Park. In 1870 construction started on a bridge to connect New York with Brooklyn, by then a town in its own right. The invention of the elevator made it possible to put up "skyscrapers" eight or ten storeys high.

In 1898 New York (from then on known as Manhattan), Brooklyn, Queens, the Bronx and Staten Island amalgamated into Greater New York with a population of more than 3 million. The early years of the 20th century saw the first genuine skyscrapers: the Flatiron Building (1902) reached a height of 286 feet with 21 floors. In 1904 the first subway line opened. Greenwich Village, which became a centre for artists, writers and theatre people, acquired a reputation for bohemianism. Following World War I, the exclusive shops and more fashionable department stores moved to Fifth Avenue, above 34th Street, and New York had to cope with traffic jams.

In October 1929 the business boom burst with the catastrophic crash of the stock market. Breadlines and jobless apple sellers became a common sight, and a shantytown sprang up in Central Park. In 1934 a dynamic mayor by the name of Fiorello La Guardia fought for public welfare measures and civic reform. He rebuilt much of the Lower East Side, but not, unfortunately, Harlem, which became the overpopulated home of not only the blacks but also the Puerto Ricans who arrived in the last wave of immigration.

World City

When the United Nations set up its headquarters in New York after World War II, the town started calling itself "World City". It's an apt title. Ever since the first settlers disembarked here, New York has been the most cosmopolitan of cities. Neighbourhoods change abruptly with a casual crossing of streets. Dialects, languages, costumes and cuisines abound in endless variety. Several foreign-language papers are still published here as each community tries to retain its individuality. Every ethnic group has its own special reason to parade along Fifth Avenue. And despite the occasional unsteadiness of world financial markets, New York remains a symbol of strength in its diversity and economic opportunity.

Overleaf: The Empire State Building offers a bird's-eye view of Manhattan's concrete canyons.

WHAT TO SEE

The real New York, of course, includes more than Manhattan. The boroughs of Brooklyn, Queens, Staten Island and the Bronx are important elements in the city's life. But the average tourist with a limited amount of time for sightseeing wants to hit the highlights. And there's no denying that Manhattan—the island queen of the metropolis, 13½ miles long and 2 miles wide—is where to find the top sights.

MIDTOWN

Most hotels are located in midtown, right in the centre of Manhattan. If this is where you're staying, you'll have no difficulty in getting around the immediate area on foot.

Here begins the slowest, priciest and most romantic sightseeing trip in Central Park.

Rockefeller Center

The original 14 buildings of this famous midtown complex cover 12 acres between Fifth Avenue and Avenue of the Americas (Sixth Avenue) from West 48th to 51st streets. Today, however, Rockefeller Center encompasses some 22 acres which include the skyscrapers on the west side of Avenue of the Americas from West 47th Street, all linked by underground concourses with shops, cafés, restaurants, a post office and the New York City subway.

When Columbia University acquired the site in 1811, it consisted of farmlands and a botanical garden. Towards the end of the century the district became quite fashionable, and handsome private homes were built. Then, during Prohibition, speakeasies (clandestine bars) moved in and Columbia had trouble finding tenants. In 1928 John D. Rockefeller asked the university for a lease on the site to raise a new commercial complex. Built between 1931 and 1940, the construction created new jobs for unemployed New Yorkers during the Depression. Now Rockefeller Center incorporates multinational enterprises and attracts thousands of visitors and shoppers daily. It's so central to the essence of New York—and America—that uproar was heard when the complex was bought by Japan's Mitsubishi group.

From Fifth Avenue you enter by the **Channel Gardens**, a pedestrian alley with fountains and flower beds. In keeping with their name, the gardens separate the Maison Française and the British Empire Building. At the end is the **Lower Plaza**, parasoled garden restaurant in summer, ice-skating rink in winter. Watched over by a gold-leaf covered statue of

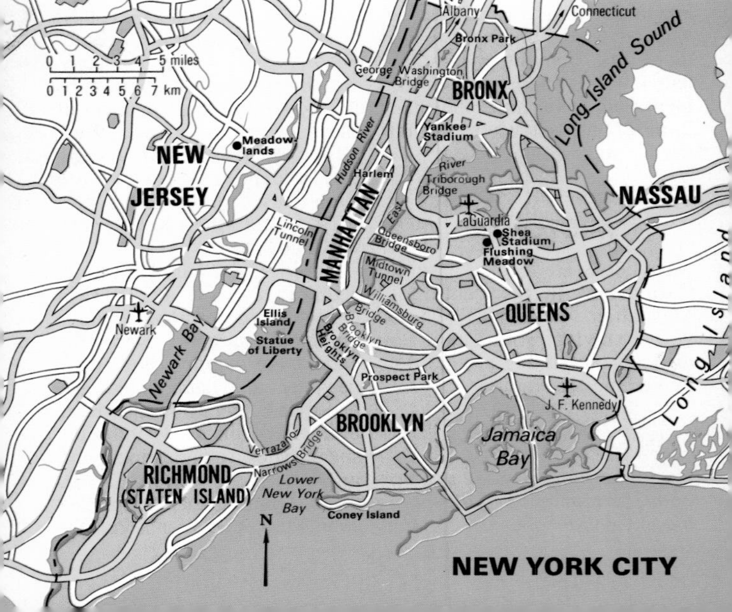

Prometheus, the plaza is dominated by the Center's main tower, the RCA Building.

A free walking tour brochure, available at the main information desk in the lobby at 30 Rockefeller Plaza, will guide you through most of the Center. On the concourse level (open weekdays), a video covers the Center's history, art, design and buildings.

On the 65th floor of the **RCA Building** (now the General Electric Building) is the **Rainbow Room**, an Art-Deco supper club with fabulous views of the city. Several floors of the RCA Building are occupied by NBC, the radio and television network. A fascinating tour behind the scenes of the broadcasting studios starts at 30 Rockefeller Plaza (Mon.–Sat. 9.30 or 10 a.m.–4 or 4.30 p.m.; children under six are not permitted).

Radio City Music Hall, at Avenue of the Americas and

FINDING YOUR WAY AROUND

It's virtually impossible to get lost in Manhattan: no other town in the world is built on such simple lines. The backbone of the island is Fifth Avenue; all areas to the west of it as far as the Hudson River are known as the "West Side", while the "East Side" covers the area between Fifth Avenue and the East River. Fifth Avenue begins at Washington Square in Greenwich Village.

"16 West 53rd Street", for example, is the address of a building on 53rd Street, just west of Fifth Avenue. You'll often hear people say "That's three blocks away". (A block is a group of buildings surrounded on four sides by streets and/or avenues.) And it's quite common to give an address as the point where two roads meet: "Fifth Avenue at 74th Street", or simply—"at 60th and Lexington".

Apart from the Wall Street area and Greenwich Village, where the streets have names and still follow the lines laid down in colonial days, all roads join at right angles and all streets are numbered. Avenues (First to Twelfth) run north–south, streets (1st to 220th) run east–west. Some of the avenues have names instead of numbers—Lexington, Madison, Park and Avenue of the Americas (colloquially Sixth Avenue). Broadway is the only one that doesn't follow a straight line.

Downtown means Manhattan south of 34th Street. Midtown speaks for itself. Uptown is the area north of 59th Street.

Incidentally, Americans refer to the ground floor as the first, and few buildings, believe it or not, have a 13th floor.

West 50th Street (normal guided tour: Mon.–Sat. 10.15 a.m.–4.45 p.m.; Sun. 11.15 a.m.–4.45 p.m.), is the largest indoor movie theatre in the world with a seating capacity of around 6,000. A symbol of the period when everything Americans did had to be better and above all bigger, Radio City holds all the records: the largest Wurlitzer organ in the world, the biggest chandeliers, a revolving stage on three levels, plus lounges downstairs decorated in the most extravagant 1930s Art-Deco style.

If you have a spare evening be sure to take in one of the seasonal shows. You'll be able to hear the famous organ and Radio City's own symphony orchestra. Featured performers at the Music Hall are the Rockettes, since 1926 America's most famous troupe of dancing girls. Hour-long backstage tours of the Hall revolve around show schedules; call the tour desk on 632-4041 for current hours.

Emerging from Radio City, you have a marvellous view of the most attractive ensemble of modern skyscrapers in New York. To the north, on the opposite side of Avenue of the Americas, stands Burlington House (between West 54th and 55th streets), then the New York Hilton (between West 53rd and 54th streets) and, in turn, the Crédit Lyonnais, Paine Webber, Time & Life (across from Radio City), Exxon, McGraw-Hill and Celanese buildings.

For a break on a hot summer's day, cross Avenue of the Americas from Radio City and walk one block down West 50th Street to take in the refreshing sight (on your left) of the Exxon Park waterfall and listen to a lunch-time musical performance. If you continue through Exxon Park across West 49th Street, you'll reach the equally delightful waterfall of the McGraw-Hill park (the water comes from the building's air-conditioning system).

Fifth Avenue

Fifth Avenue suggests luxury not just in the States but all over the world. It used to be the home of millionaires who lived between 34th and 50th streets until around 1900, when they started moving to Central Park, making way for fancy stores. The most exclusive are to be

Trump Tower's atrium is the perfect place to avoid sunstroke—or a blizzard.

found between 39th and 58th streets—the luxury department stores: Saks Fifth Avenue (at East 50th Street), Henri Bendel (between West 55th and 56th streets), Bergdorf Goodman (between West 57th and 58th streets); the jewellers: Cartier (at East 52nd Street), Tiffany & Co. (at East 57th Street), Van Cleef & Arpels (at West 57th Street); the shops of Trump Tower (at East 56th Street); boutiques of the top couturiers; the famous leather-goods stores; and a number of excellent bookshops. A bit further down, West 47th Street between Fifth and Sixth avenues is called the "Diamond Jewelry Way". It is well worth a detour for its glittering window displays and a look at the colourful people involved in the gem trade.

St. Patrick's Cathedral (between East 50th and 51st streets), built in 1858–74 as an imitation of Cologne's Gothic cathedral, is a little lost today among the skyscrapers of Rockefeller Center and the Olympic Tower next door. Seat of the Archdiocese of New York, the church comes into its own on the occasion of the Irish Catholic parade on St. Patrick's Day, March 17.

The **Grand Army Plaza**, in the corner of Central Park South (at West 59th Street), marks the division between the shopping area of Fifth Avenue and the residential section, lined with mansions and de luxe apartment buildings. You'll pass by here on your way to one of the nearby museums. This is the place to hire a horse-drawn carriage for a ride around Central Park (see pp. 54–58). It's also the site of two of New York's smartest hotels, the Plaza and the Pierre (at East 61st Street). Across from the Plaza, set a little way back from the avenue, is the General Motors headquarters, a modern skyscraper designed by Edward Stone.

Take a look, too, at the succession of skyscrapers along Madison Avenue, one block east of Fifth Avenue—especially the IBM Building (at East 56th Street), which links up to Trump Tower on Fifth Avenue. Next door is AT&T's controversial postmodernist World Headquarters, which houses the **AT&T InfoQuest Center**, a museum focusing on telecommunication technology. The 57-storey tower of the Helmsley Palace hotel (between East 50th and 51st streets) incorporates the neo-Renaissance **Villard Houses**, a New York landmark since 1885.

Times Square and Broadway

Times Square, stretching from the north side of West 42nd Street up to Duffy Square at West 47th Street, got its name from *The New York Times*, which set up office here in 1904. It's the heart of the Theater District, with first-run cinemas, playhouses, restaurants, nightclubs, hotels and shops. But the area also has some of the city's nastiest strip clubs and sex shops. The night scene reveals sleek limousines depositing ladies in evening dress just up the street from prostitutes and drug dealers.

Everybody has seen pictures of the moving illuminated news tape at **One Times Square**, made up of more than 12,000 electric light bulbs. On December 31 a lighted globe comes down a pole on the top of the building, announcing the arrival of the New Year. Tens of thousands of people come to witness the event, which is also shown on television.

Not all activity in Times Square is above ground. Underneath, where several subway lines converge, professional musicians entertain the travelling crowds.

The metaphor for the New York Theatre is **Broadway**. The city's biggest shows (at the highest prices) are put on in a handful of auditoriums on Broadway itself, like the Winter Garden (1634 Broadway), but most "On-Broadway" plays are performed at the theatres on its side streets between West 44th and 53rd streets and at Lincoln Center. **Off-Broadway** theatres, with auditoriums of 100 to 499 seats, and **Off-Off-Broadway** theatres, with fewer than 100 seats, charge lower prices; these descriptions have nothing to do with geographical location, they merely differentiate between mainstream and offbeat, less commercial productions. (See THEATRE, pp. 85–86.)

Musical history has been made since the 1890s in **Carnegie Hall** (Seventh Avenue at West 57th Street), where backstage tours are offered on Tuesdays and Thursdays.

42nd Street

West of Times Square, 42nd Street is known as "Sin Street". But the area is being redeveloped and dramatically upgraded, the horror-and-porno movie houses giving way to legitimate theatre. Going east, by contrast, it has always been

cameras
Capezio
POST
NO BIL

one of the most fascinating streets in the midtown area, the place for pace-setting buildings: here you'll see some of the great successes in the history of American architecture.

At West 42nd Street and Sixth Avenue are two attractive skyscrapers, both completed in 1974: the **New York Telephone Company Building** on the corner—all white marble and black glass—and the **W.R. Grace Building** between Fifth and Sixth avenues, with its striking, slightly concave silhouette. The same architect, Gordon Bunshaft, designed an almost identical building on 57th Street, a few steps from Fifth Avenue. Both are really magnificent.

Bryant Park occupies the site of the Crystal Palace, built for the 1853 World's Fair and destroyed by fire six years later. The park, not recommended after dark, lies behind the **New York Public Library**. This monument in American Beaux-Arts style (neoclassic) opened in 1911; two well-photographed stone lions guard the entrance. One of the largest libraries in the world, it possesses several million books, almost as many manuscripts, and vast reading rooms; it's a favourite with browsers and serious researchers alike. A number of rare works are put on display in turn. Changing exhibitions are held in Gottesman Hall (free entry; closed Sundays and public holidays).

Further east on 42nd Street, blocking the view up Park Avenue, is the massive bulk of **Grand Central Station**, completed in 1913. Inside, 66 rail lines arrive on the upper level, 57 on the lower. The central concourse, one of the largest in the world, is invaded every afternoon from 4 to 5.30 p.m. by hundreds of thousands of suburban commuters catching their trains home. New Yorkers either love or hate the place, and attempts have been made more than once to have it torn down. It is now classified as a national monument, another example of the Beaux-Arts style.

A network of passageways links Grand Central to nearby hotels, office buildings and the subway. They're lined with all

In cosmopolitan New York even chess is an outdoor sport.

kinds of shops and several restaurants including the venerable **Oyster Bar & Restaurant**, a New York institution.

Directly behind the station is the **Pan Am Building**, the head office of the airline, where more than 20,000 people work. Cutting across Park Avenue, the 59-floor octagonal structure is easily recognized, even from afar. Escalators lead down to Grand Central Station.

Landmarks on Park Avenue north of Grand Central and the Pan Am Building include the **Waldorf-Astoria** hotel (between East 49th and 50th streets), host to distinguished personalities since 1931, and the bronze-and-glass **Seagram Building** (between East 52nd and 53rd streets), a 1958 pace-setter by Mies van der Rohe and Philip Johnson.

Around the corner the **Citicorp Center** (East 53rd Street between Lexington and Third avenues) brings a rich touch to the skyline with its dramatically sloping silver roof. At ground level is a lively three-storey "market" of shops and restaurants around a sky-lit central courtyard and the free-standing polygonal **St. Peter's Church**, with a lovely chapel decorated by Louise Nevelson.

Back on East 42nd Street, gawk at the **Chrysler Building**. When completed in 1930 this was the tallest skyscraper in the world, but in a matter of months it was overtaken by the Empire State Building. Chrysler is a positive temple to the automobile: the top is shaped like the radiator cap on Chrysler's 1929 model and the façade is dotted with stylized automobile motifs. Although architecturally one of the most original efforts in New York, it is now just another office building.

At the corner of Second Avenue stands the Art-Deco **News Building**, home of the *Daily News,* a pioneering mass-circulation tabloid. An enormous revolving globe occupies a good part of the lobby.

Further on, between First and Second avenues, you will pass the offices of the Ford Foundation, with a marvellous interior **garden** (open weekdays 9 a.m.–5 p.m.).

Taking it easy on the steps of the New York Public Library; inside, researchers are burrowing through more than 5 million books.

Bud

William Van Alen designed the Chrysler Building as a fitting monument to Walter Percy Chrysler's achievements in the automobile industry. It was to be the highest office block in the world. However, during its construction it was challenged by the Bank of the Manhattan Co. Building, whose architect added a flagpole, thus overtaking the Chrysler Building by two feet. Van Alen countered this move by adding a spire, making the Chrysler Building 1,046 feet tall when completed in 1930. After this bitter fight the Chrysler Building was only in the book of records for a few months—in 1931 it was surpassed by the Empire State Building.

The United Nations

John D. Rockefeller, Jr. donated the 18-acre site in order to persuade the members of the UN to set up their headquarters in New York. A team of 11 architects, including the American Wallace K. Harrison, the Swiss Le Corbusier and the Brazilian Oscar Niemeyer, designed the buildings, completed in the early 1950s. The **Secretariat** is housed in the tower, and the **General Assembly** meets in the lower block with the slightly concave roof. The complex includes two other buildings: the **Dag Hammarskjöld Library** (a memorial to the former Secretary General) and the **Conference Building**. The view of the UN complex is more spectacular from the river (or Queens) than from First Avenue.

Only a few rooms in the Secretariat are open to the public, but when the General Assembly is in session, visitors can usually attend meetings. Obtain a ticket from the information desk in the lobby (East 46th Street and First Avenue). This is also the starting point for **guided tours** (daily 9.15 a.m.–4.45 p.m.; Jan.–Feb. weekdays 9.15 a.m.–4.45 p.m.). The tour, which lasts an hour, takes you behind the scenes and explains how the UN works. Most member states have donated works of art which are on display in the Conference Building. These include Persian rugs, North African mosaics and a Chagall stained-glass panel, among other treasures. The Security Council Room was a gift from Norway, the Trusteeship Council Room from Denmark and the Economic and Social Council Room from Sweden.

On weekdays visitors can have an early lunch in the **Delegates' Dining Room** overlooking the East River (bring your passport or other piece of identification). It's advisable to reserve your table at the information desk in the lobby. Less formal is the coffee shop in the central hall on the lower level. There's a shop specializing in crafts from all over the world, where you can find original gifts at reasonable prices. The bookshop sells UN publications, and stamp collectors shouldn't miss the post office which sells UN stamps. However, they are only valid for letters and cards posted within the complex. After your tour, you can relax in the 18-acre grounds overlooking the East River and Queens.

Empire State Building

It's no longer the tallest building in the world, and Americans tend to exaggerate when they call it "the cathedral of the skies" or "the eighth wonder of the world". But it's something you shouldn't miss—unless, of course, it's a foggy day. At Fifth Avenue and West 34th Street, the Empire State Building is open to the public every day from 9.30 a.m. until midnight. Everything about it is huge: 102 storeys; 60,000 tons of steel; 3,500 miles of telephone wires and cables; 60 miles of pipes; a volume of 1¼ million cubic yards; 1,860 steps; and, last but not least, a height of 1,454 feet (including the television tower and antenna).

To reach the **observation deck** you first have to go down to the basement level. There you buy your ticket and get in line. Next to the ticket office why not take a look at the **Guinness World of Records** exhibition? The museum features life-size displays of world-record holders, videos, a data bank on sports, space, science and music superlatives, as well as a ten-foot sculpture of New York landmarks.

An elevator will speed you up to the 80th floor in less than a minute. You'll just have time to catch your breath and get your ears unblocked before taking a second elevator to the 86th floor—1,050 feet above street level. In winter you can stay inside the heated shelter of the observatory. In summer enjoy the **view** from the outside terrace. On a clear day you can make out the funnels of ships 40 miles out at sea.

If you're not discouraged by the line of people, you can take a third elevator right up to the observatory on the 102nd floor. There you will be at the foot of the 204-foot-high communications tower and antenna, from which television and FM radio stations transmit programmes to the metropolitan area.

Back on earth, the area near the Empire State Building contains some of New York's most popular stores. Go west along 34th Street for Macy's and the A & S Plaza (see WHEN AND WHERE TO SHOP, pp. 82–83). Nearby, at Seventh Avenue and West 33rd Street, is **Madison Square Garden**, renowned for boxing matches and various entertainment attractions including the circus. In addition to being home to the New York Knickerbockers ("Knicks"—basketball) and the Rangers (hockey), it is also used as a

conference centre. The Garden seats 20,000 people and the Felt Forum can take an additional 5,000.

Below Madison Square Garden is Pennsylvania Station (invariably referred to as Penn Station), the railway terminal for Long Island and New Jersey commuters.

The former Penn Central railway yard is now the site of the city's newest convention centre: a sensational glass structure named after a feisty New Yorker, long-time Senator Jacob Javits.

DOWNTOWN

Wall Street Area

The Financial District, located at the southern tip of Manhattan, is in some respects the most impressive part of New York. Here you really feel you're at the very heart of the world's greatest power. The skyscrapers, closer together than elsewhere, look all the more massive, and the streets are veritable canyons.

Wall Street itself got its name from the stockade (really a wall of boards) built here in 1653 by the Dutch governor Peter Stuyvesant to protect New Amsterdam from the Indians. It didn't do much good because the settlers persisted in carting off planks for their own uses. Today no address anywhere holds greater prestige.

At the junction of Wall and Nassau streets is the **Federal Hall National Memorial** (open weekdays 9 a.m.–5 p.m.). The original building, demolished in 1812, was the home of the United States Congress for a year. On April 30, 1789, George Washington took the oath here as the first president of the United States.

The **New York Stock Exchange**, across the way, is the largest in the United States; you don't have to be an investor to find the place exciting. The entrance at 20 Broad Street leads into the visitors' gallery, open during most of the Exchange's trading hours (weekdays 9.15 a.m.–4 p.m.). From there you'll have a bird's-eye view of the controlled chaos of the trading floor. You can learn about the workings of the

In New York's parks and squares, you can get away from the hustle and bustle of street life.

Exchange from a permanent exhibit and a film. A demonstration of the famous ticker tape is also featured.

After the stress and strain of the stock market, relax for a bit in one of the coolest spots in Manhattan—**Battery Park**, on the southern tip of the island. You have a splendid view of New York Bay. The round fortress on the water is **Castle Clinton** (open daily 8.30 a.m.–5 p.m.). Built in 1811 but never used for military purposes, it was later converted to a theatre and renamed Castle Garden. Lafayette was received here with great ceremony in 1825. From 1855 to 1890 Castle Garden served as an immigration reception centre: 7 million Europeans passed through this building. Until 1941 it housed an aquarium. Now classified as a historical monument, Castle Clinton has been restored to its original state and name, and contains a small museum.

To the north-west of the park is the southern tip of Battery Park City (see p. 43). The **Old Custom House** (the new one is located in the World Trade Center; see pp. 39–43), facing neighbouring Bowling Green, stands on the site of an old fort where, it's said, Peter Minuit bought Manhattan from the Indians for $24 (at 1626 prices). The present column-and-statuary-studded edifice was built in 1907. The four sculptures at its base represent Asia, America, Europe and Africa.

On the corner of Pearl and Broad streets stands **Fraunces Tavern**, built as a home in 1719 then converted to a tavern in 1763 by Samuel Fraunces. It was here, in the Long Room, that George Washington bade his officers farewell on December 4, 1783, after the Revolutionary War was won. Now it houses the **Fraunces Tavern Museum** (open weekdays 10 a.m.–4 p.m.), which features exhibits on the Revolutionary War and 18th-century American history and culture, and a regular programme of lectures and concerts.

Across Water Street, behind the old tavern and dwarfed by towering skyscrapers, the attractively laid out Vietnam Veterans Plaza opens onto the East River. In its centre stands the evocative **Vietnam Veterans Memorial**, a 66-foot-long and 16-foot-high granite-and-glass block etched with quotations from letters and diaries written by U.S. soldiers during their service, as well as public statements about the war.

Returning to Nassau Street,

behind Federal Hall you can admire the shining glass and aluminium tower of the **Chase Manhattan Bank**, built in 1961. About 15,000 people work in this 65-storey structure. The plaza leading to the building contains some modern statues by the Japanese sculptor Isamu Noguchi and the Frenchman Jean Dubuffet.

The Episcopalian **Trinity Church** at Broadway and Wall Street was built in 1846 in neo-Gothic style with bronze doors copied from the Baptistry in Florence. Some 280 feet high, the spire holds a bell dating from the 18th century. In the adjacent cemetery you can see the graves of many illustrious Americans including Alexander Hamilton, one of the Founding Fathers, and Robert Fulton, inventor of the steamboat. Trinity Church is one of New York's richest landlords, with extensive holdings going back to colonial times.

A little further uptown, between Broadway and Park Row, **City Hall**, built between 1803 and 1812, is still greatly admired for its elegant architecture. The offices of the Mayor of New York ("Hizzoner", as the tabloids call him) are located here. There's also an interesting collection of portraits and furniture from the federal period (open weekdays 9 a.m.–6 p.m.).

You need no directions to find the twin towers of the **World Trade Center**: they're visible all over town. Not (quite) the tallest buildings in the world, the figures are nonetheless impressive: 1,350 feet high with 43,600 windows. Each tower has 23 express and 72 local elevators, as well as four for freight. The whole Center covers an area of 16 acres. It is served by various subway lines including the PATH system under the Hudson to New Jersey, which disgorges tens of thousands of commuters every morning. The stations are accessible from the concourse (street) level, the site of a vast shopping centre and numerous restaurants.

Even if your time in New York is limited, try to fit in a visit to the top of the World Trade Center. The **observation deck** (open daily 9.30 a.m.–9.30 p.m.; in summer daily 9.30 a.m.–11.30 p.m.) on the 107th floor of 2 World Trade Center dominates the city. And,

Overleaf: Swinging 1,350 feet below the swaying World Trade Center.

EAST

weather permitting, you can go even higher—to the **open-air rooftop promenade** above the 110th floor, the highest outdoor observation platform in the world. The famous restaurant **Windows on the World** is located on the 107th floor of 1 World Trade Center.

The Port Authority of New York and New Jersey was responsible for building the Center, inaugurated in 1970. In addition to the two towers with their thousands of offices, there are five lower buildings in the complex, including a 22-storey hotel. A gigantic bronze fountain globe highlights the central square, the stage for free noontime summer concerts.

The 30 million cubic feet of earth and rocks excavated from the site were dumped into the Hudson River adjacent to the Trade Center. They created a 23-acre landfill which is now part of the **Battery Park City**—a spacious area dotted with greenery, high- and low-rise luxury apartment houses and office buildings. The centrepiece of the "city" is the striking **World Financial Center**, four towers and a huge Winter Garden crowned by a vaulted glass ceiling. Shops, bars, cafés and restaurants occupy the first two floors of the buildings, where free concerts and a range of other events take place throughout the year.

Fritz Koenig's 25-foot-high globe in the World Trade Center Plaza.

Redevelopment in the 1970s and early '80s changed the face of **South Street Seaport**, a historic enclave on the East River just south-west of Brooklyn Bridge. Site of the country's busiest port from 1800 to 1870, today's Seaport comprises 11 blocks of buildings, both old and new, packed with cafés and restaurants, boutiques, stores and separate food and wholesale fish markets. There's diversion in the form of historic ships, a theatre, museum galleries, free open-air concerts and street performers.

The centre's cultural nerve is the **South Street Seaport Museum**, dispersed over several blocks, which offers tours and visits to the galleries and ships. Star among the vessels is the four-masted barge *Peking,* dating from 1911, tied up at Pier 16. From here, too, you can take harbour cruises on replicas of 19th-century river boats.

Lower East Side

At the turn of the century, during the flood of immigration, throngs of newcomers moved into the Lower East Side. The vast majority of them stayed only a few years, long enough to learn English, find a job and then set off to make a living elsewhere in the United States.

But substantial groups of Chinese, Jews and Italians chose to settle a little longer in their own enclaves. The Chinese are still here in strength, and the colours, sounds and smells of the other communities also linger on.

If you take the subway to **Chinatown**, you won't go wrong: the Canal Street Station has signs in both Roman and Chinese characters. The telephone booths have pagoda roofs, narrow shops sell ivory and jade jewellery, grocers display Chinese cabbage, winter melon and snow peas, and countless restaurants feature Cantonese, Shanghai and Szechwan specialities.

Well over 100,000 Chinese live in Chinatown, a loosely defined area centred around Canal Street, Mott Street and Chatham Square. The earliest arrivals came to the country during the California Gold Rush and period of railway construction in the 19th century; most of the immigrants today come directly from Hong Kong. To learn about the history and sites of the area, take the daily hour-long walking tour conducted by the New York Chinatown History Project (tel. 619-4785).

Join the Chinese from the rest of New York, who come here at weekends to do their shopping and enjoy a meal out.

Forming an intersection of ten streets in the southern part of Chinatown, the adjoining Chatham and Kimlau squares are chaotic in both vehicular and pedestrian traffic. At the corner of the Bowery (see p. 50) and Division Street stands a 1983 bronze statue of **Confucius**, and south of the squares, a few steps down St. James Place, are New York's oldest "monuments", barely a dozen effaced but touching tombstones, the remnants of the **Shearith Israel Cemetery**, founded here in 1656 by Spanish and Portuguese Jews.

You can make your Garden of Paradise in the Lower East Side.

品大酒樓
新合興

Even tinier than its name suggests, **Little Italy** is centred on Mulberry Street a few blocks to the north-west—and shares its southern part with Chinatown. The Italian section is now principally a gastronomic hub, with expensive as well as moderately priced restaurants and espresso bars, high-quality caterers and, scattered among them, souvenir shops and the occasional grocery store specializing in home-made and imported Italian delicacies. The street is at its liveliest during the ten-day Feast of San Gennaro, which takes place in September.

The remnants of the old **Jewish quarter** are located on the north-east side of Chinatown, beyond Hester Street, which was the site of the Jewish market at the end of the 19th century. Follow Hester Street eastwards and then walk north along **Orchard Street** and you'll see a shadow of the market's heyday, but such a lively shadow that you sense how hectic it once was. Dormant on the Sabbath from Friday evening to Saturday at sunset, the place springs to life on Sundays when Orthodox Jews in black hats and long, black frock coats pick their way among Hispanic and black vendors. The clothes stores and delicatessens ring with accents inherited from the Jewish villages of Polish Galicia and the Ukraine. For a snack, have a bulging pastrami (seasoned smoked beef) sandwich and a cup of lemon tea in one of the kosher dairy restaurants.

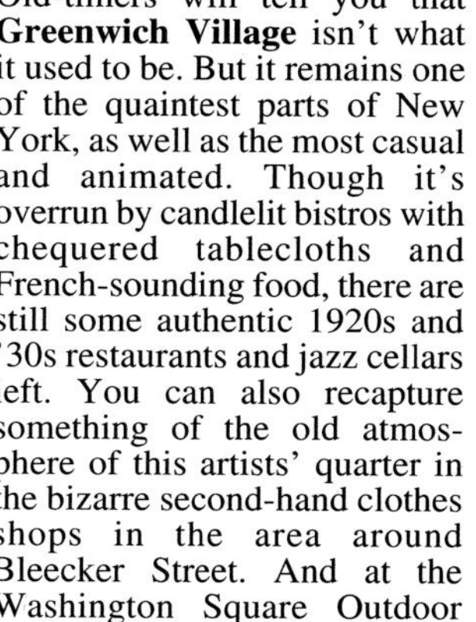

The exuberance of an outdoor market in Chinatown.

Atmospheric Neighbourhoods

Old-timers will tell you that **Greenwich Village** isn't what it used to be. But it remains one of the quaintest parts of New York, as well as the most casual and animated. Though it's overrun by candlelit bistros with chequered tablecloths and French-sounding food, there are still some authentic 1920s and '30s restaurants and jazz cellars left. You can also recapture something of the old atmosphere of this artists' quarter in the bizarre second-hand clothes shops in the area around Bleecker Street. And at the Washington Square Outdoor Art Exhibit, a summertime tradition since 1931, hundreds of painters, sculptors and photographers display their works.

The boundaries of Greenwich Village run north–south from 14th Street to Houston Street and east–west from Broadway to the Hudson River. Its most famous landmark is the **Washington Arch** in Washington Square at the foot of Fifth Avenue. Designed by Stanford White, this triumphal arch was erected in 1889 to mark the centenary of George Washington's inauguration as president.

Washington Square Park—now notorious for its drug dealers—remains the heart of the New York University campus. It's surrounded by university buildings with classrooms and student residences; the elegant old houses on the north side are the homes of professors. Hidden away behind these dwellings are two private lanes that used to lead to the stables belonging to Washington Square's wealthy inhabitants: **Washington Mews**, one block up Fifth Avenue on your right, and **MacDougal Alley**, a few steps up MacDougal Street from the north-western end of the square.

Any of the narrow streets to the west and south merits a visit. Walk west along 8th Street across Avenue of the Americas to Christopher Street and into a charming residential area of small tree-lined streets of "brownstones"—matching brick or brownish-red sandstone houses, each with a flight of stairs leading up to the door. Some of the Village's best antique dealers are clustered here, as well as some good restaurants.

Follow Bleecker Street to the south-east. This is the main shopping strip of the neighbourhood, teeming with quaint little craft and curio shops, cafés and small restaurants.

You should make at least two trips to the Village—by day to see the sights and at night to catch the atmosphere, have dinner and listen to some jazz.

SoHo (short for South of Houston Street) is the quarter bounded by Houston Street, Broadway, Canal Street and the river. It has become the Village's chic southern neighbour, with expensive cafés, restaurants and art galleries, and boutiques selling the very latest in fashion.

Its history has followed the pattern of the Village. Artists who couldn't afford the rents after the Village's commercialization moved south to the abandoned lofts and warehouse floors of the industrial district of SoHo. The most successful of them were able to install kitchens, bathrooms and comfortable interiors. Others made do with bare walls and floors for the sake of ample space and light. But with the success of the avant-garde galleries on West Broadway—especially No. 420, where the old pillars of the pop art movement, Andy Warhol, Robert Rauschenberg and Roy Lichtenstein displayed their works—rents soared. Interior decorators and gallery owners took over and turned the lofts and ground floors into expensive residential and commercial properties. The gentry moved in, and the artists moved out, many of them heading south-west to the dilapidated warehouses of the **TriBeCa** (Triangle Below Canal Street) quarter.

So close to the modern Financial District of the World Trade Center and Battery Park City with all its glitter and wealth, TriBeCa, too, has become a favoured area, and art galleries, trendy restaurants and boutiques have duly blossomed.

The **East Village** extends from Broadway eastward to First Avenue and beyond. Much less affluent than its big

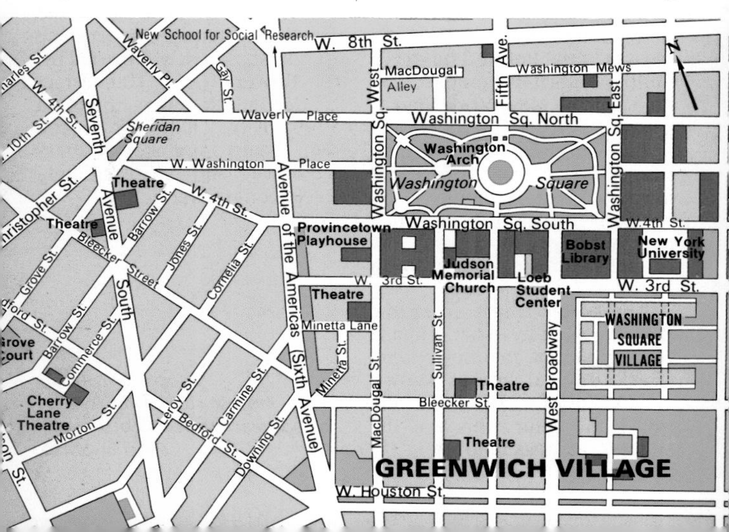

brother to the west, this neighbourhood nevertheless has its share of avant-garde galleries, new-wave clothes shops, night spots and small ethnic restaurants. In fact, purists claim this is the *real* Village. Through the curtainless windows of its back streets, you can glimpse paintings or sculpture in the making.

From Broadway, the stubby but spacious **Astor Place** leads on to Cooper Square and St. Mark's Place—strange that the eastern part of this area hasn't been dubbed "Little Poland". At Lafayette Street, just south of Cooper Square, stands the building which once housed the first public library. Today it's the seat of the **Public Theater**, a multi-auditorium complex and home of the New York Shakespeare Festival. The traditional and avant-garde theatre and film shows presented here are always of high quality, and some plays tentatively launched here went on to become the longest running shows on Broadway.

Across the street from the theatre you'll see what remains of a group of marble-pillared Greek Revival houses known as **Colonnade Row**. In the mid-19th century this was the smartest address in town.

A few blocks south, Great Jones Street eastwards leads on to the **Bowery**, laid out by Peter Stuyvesant in the 17th century as the road to his farm (*bouwerij* in Dutch). In the 19th century this was New York's "grand boulevard" lined with dance halls and beer taverns. These days it's mostly given over to sordid hotels and the occasional drunk. But there are some good rock and jazz spots, and theatres have moved in. You needn't be afraid to go there in the evening: the Bowery is much less dangerous than it looks.

And a final downtown church: on the spot where the Stuyvesant family chapel once stood, **St. Mark's Church in-the-Bowery** (East 10th Street at Second Avenue), built in 1799, is a charming church with noteworthy stained-glass windows—and an extremely lively congregation.

Shops range from the luxurious Fifth Avenue department stores to a souvenir shop in SoHo.

DON'T WORRY
BE HAPPY
NEW YORK CITY
NEW YORK CITY
NEW YORK CITY
BLUES

UPTOWN

The Upper West Side is the area of Manhattan west of Central Park. It's a lively mixed-up district, the part of town that can claim most success in racial integration. Here a hodgepodge of intellectuals and artists live side by side with shopkeepers and bus drivers of different ethnic and racial backgrounds. In and around Columbus Avenue between Lincoln Center and West 79th Street, prestigious stores, boutiques, restaurants, popular art galleries and antique shops have taken over from the old neighbourhood establishments.

Lincoln Center

It was construction of the Lincoln Center for the Performing Arts, between 62nd and 66th streets west of Broadway, that launched the revival of this neighbourhood. In 1955 John D. Rockefeller III put forward the proposal for a great cultural centre to house the Metropolitan Opera, the New York Philharmonic, the New York City Ballet and the Juilliard School of Music. The city bought the land and razed the Puerto Rican ghetto on the site. Financed entirely by private funds, the Center covers an area of some 12 acres. The plaza, an esplanade surrounding a fountain, is the focal point of the three major buildings, each designed by a different architect to blend harmoniously with the others.

To the left of the plaza is the **New York State Theater**, home of the New York City Ballet and the New York City Opera. Designed by Philip Johnson and built in 1964, it has a simple, stately façade but a lush, red and gold auditorium studded with crystal.

The **Metropolitan Opera House** (the "Met"), host to the Metropolitan Opera and the American Ballet Theatre, was designed by Wallace K. Harrison, completed in 1966 and can hold 3,800 people. It is the most beautiful building in the complex, with an airy front of glass highlighted by marble pillars, reminiscent of American colonial style. Two Chagall murals adorning the central lobby can be seen from the outside. During the summer, the Guggenheim Bandshell in

After an evening at the ballet, New York revellers can't resist taking to the floor themselves.

the adjacent Damrosch Park is the scene of open-air concerts.

Facing the New York State Theater is **Avery Fisher Hall**, completed in 1962, also known as Philharmonic Hall. The auditorium, which seats approximately 2,700, was refinished to provide excellent acoustics. The New York Philharmonic and distinguished visiting orchestras and soloists play here.

Just behind the hall, level with the Met, you can see the outline of the **Vivian Beaumont Theater**, designed by the great architect Eero Saarinen who died before its completion in 1965. In addition to the delightful circular theatre, there is the second, much smaller, **Mitzi Newhouse Theater**. The building was originally intended to provide a base for a permanent American repertory company, along the lines of the Comédie Française in Paris, but the dream never materialized.

Behind the Vivian Beaumont, the **New York Public Library and Museum of the Performing Arts at Lincoln Center** includes a film archive and a file on actors, film stars and directors. Further back, but connected to Lincoln Center by a foot-bridge over West 65th Street, you'll find the **Juilliard School**, one of the world's outstanding conservatories of music. **Alice Tully Hall** on the ground floor is a concert hall where the best pupils often perform in afternoon concerts. It is also the home of the Chamber Music Society.

One-hour guided tours of Lincoln Center start from the concourse daily from 10 a.m. to 5 p.m.

Central Park

A vast green breathing space in the centre of Manhattan (half a mile wide and 2½ miles long), Central Park is sports field, playground and picnic spot for tens of thousands of city-dwellers. In the 1840s the poet William Cullen Bryant realized that New York needed more parks for its rapidly expanding population. He launched a campaign to persuade the city to buy the land—then wasteland beyond the city limits, inhabited by squatters. Frederick Law Olmsted and Calvert Vaux, landscape gardeners, were called upon to design the park. It took 3,000 workers

Harmony reigns in a quiet corner of Central Park.

In Central Park there are about 9 miles of driveways, 5½ miles of bridle paths, 6¾ miles of bicycle lanes, and 28½ miles of walks. Apart from the park's various attractions, facilities are provided for boating, ice skating, roller skating, baseball, football, bowling, croquet, tennis, handball, and even horseshoe pitching. To entertain the kids there are a number of playgrounds, a carousel and a children's zoo.

16 years to complete it. Conceived in the English style, the park doesn't really look man-made—the Lake, the "forests", the paths and meadows might have been there since time immemorial. The 75,000 trees, flourishing despite the shortage of soil and the abundance of rocks, are home to countless half-tame squirrels.

By day it's perfectly safe to go walking in the park, but be wary of those around you. Avoid it at night, unless you're going to the outdoor summer theatre.

Starting from the south-east corner of the park, skirt the Pond to the small, modern **zoo**. Then call in at the **Dairy**, the Central Park Visitors' Center, for a calendar of park events. From here, head up the wide, tree-lined Mall to the ornamented **Bethesda Fountain and Terrace**. In summer, you can hire a rowing boat at the Loeb Boathouse—to your right—for a trip on the pretty Lake stretching out below the terrace. At the oval **Conservatory Water**, to the east, permit holders sail their miniature boats next to statues of Hans Christian Andersen and Alice in Wonderland. On a hill level with the Metropolitan Museum of Art (see pp. 64–66) stands **Cleopatra's Needle**, a 3,000-year-old obelisk that was a gift from Egypt in the late 19th century.

A more recent addition to Central Park, **Strawberry Fields** (at Central Park West between West 71st and 74th streets) was Yoko Ono's horticultural memorial to her husband, John Lennon, who was shot in 1980 just across the street, in front of the ponderous Dakota apartment house (1 West 72nd Street).

The 1½-mile path around the Reservoir is especially popular among joggers. For active sport lovers, something is going on in the park every day, but most of all on Sundays in the summer. There are miles of bicycle and jogging paths, which are turned into cross-country ski runs in winter, along with tennis courts, ice-skating rinks and adventure playgrounds for children.

Free open-air concerts and operas are presented on the **Great Lawn** during the summer months, and in **Belvedere Castle** there are exhibits and special events.

The **Delacorte Theater**, south of 81st Street on the west side of the park, is the place to see the excellent (free) Shakespeare in the Park Festival.

Columbia University Area

At Amsterdam Avenue and West 112th Street, the venerable **Cathedral Church of St. John the Divine** is "the world's largest Gothic-style cathedral". Begun in 1892 and almost completed by 1939, much remains to be done if the original plans are to be respected. Inside this Episcopalian cathedral are some beautiful tapestries, paintings by 16th-century Italian masters and several icons. The church is well known for its jazz and choral music series.

Immediately beyond the cathedral, you come to the campus of **Columbia University**. Founded by King George II in 1754 as King's College, Columbia is a member of the Ivy League, that very exclusive club of old American universities. Dwight D. Eisenhower was its president for a while after World War II. The law school, the departments of political science and education and the school of journalism all enjoy excellent reputations. You can wander around most of the campus quite freely. The Pantheon-like building with the monumental stairway on the north end of the central campus is the **Low Library**.

The university is private and, therefore, fee-paying, but its income from rented property enables it to offer a number of scholarships. The university outgrew its actual campus long ago and now owns most of the apartment houses in the neighbourhood.

Across Broadway stands **Barnard College**, Columbia University's affiliated women's college, and behind it looms the stolid Gothic **Riverside Church**. Its bell tower, housing a 74-bell carillon, offers sweeping views of New York, the Hudson River and New Jersey. The temple-like edifice in Riverside Park at West 122nd Street is **Grant's Tomb** (open from Wednesday to Sunday), the mausoleum of General Ulysses S. Grant, Commander-in-Chief of the Union Army in the Civil War and United States president from 1869 to 1877.

Beside the park is **Riverside Drive**, lined with apartment houses that started life in the luxury class, then were out of fashion for a while, but are once again very much in demand. If you want to get a good idea of life in a New York neighbourhood, walk back along Broadway until you're tired, then take the subway to your hotel.

Harlem

"Won't go to Harlem in ermine and pearls", says the old song, but that's no reason not to go at all, with the proper precautions. Of course, this place can be dangerous—a large part of it is a slum and slums everywhere tend to be dangerous. But it's also part of New York's reality. This is one time when a guided tour is highly recommended.

A drive through Harlem is included in most sightseeing tours of Manhattan. There are also a couple of agencies run by blacks who want to show their community to outsiders without concealing the worst features or overemphasizing the best. These companies offer bus and walking tours to landmarks like traditional Harlem churches, the Hamilton Grange National Memorial at Convent Avenue between West 141st and 142nd streets (home of Alexander Hamilton, leader of the Federalists and the first secretary of the Treasury), and the Morris-Jumel Mansion (see p. 61), as well as jazz, gospel and Harlem-by-night tours. For addresses, contact the New York Convention & Visitors Bureau (see p. 120) or the Harlem Visitors & Conventions Association, tel. 427-3317.

Harlem stretches from the northern reaches of Central Park up to 178th Street. In the 1950s it was the home of a million blacks from the southern states and the Caribbean. Today barely a quarter of a million remain. Optimists attribute this exodus to new housing programmes and the improvement in living standards among black people. The pessimists counterclaim that the poor have been forced out of Manhattan by the increasing dilapidation of their ghetto, and have only gone as far as outlying districts such as the South Bronx, which has become a second Harlem. There's some truth in both arguments.

Founded by Dutch settlers, Harlem remained a village for a long time. Not until the end of the 19th century was it assimilated into the town. Since the newcomers settled on the Lower East Side, middle-class Americans decided to put a gap between themselves and the people they considered ill-bred and noisy. A lot of families built second residences in Harlem, and some traces of its former glory can still be seen on the building façades.

Black people started moving in around 1920, the beginning of the Jazz Age. New York was the Promised Land for southern blacks, who found untold freedom here.

It is difficult to imagine how it was in those days. The rundown areas of today's Harlem convey the picture of a bombed-out city, the result of a cataclysmic social civil war. But signs of renewal are spreading. And the famous **Apollo Theatre** (West 125th Street between Adam Clayton Powell Jr. and Frederick Douglass boulevards) has come to life again as a combined cinema and concert hall, which is especially popular for its animated amateur night shows. The **Studio Museum in Harlem** (West 125th Street at Malcolm X Boulevard) is dedicated to the arts and artefacts of black America and the Caribbean. There are also concerts and films and a museum shop.

At Malcolm X Boulevard and West 135th Street, the **Schomburg Center for Research in Black Culture**, a public library and art museum, possesses one of the world's most important collections covering black History and African-American culture.

And some nice streets remain, particularly around Edgecombe Avenue, an area peopled by wealthy blacks who could afford to move away but have stayed out of solidarity. The **Morris-Jumel Mansion** at Jumel Terrace and West 161st Street (open Tues.–Sun. 10 a.m.–4 p.m.), a stately house set in a garden, is one of New York's last reminders of the Georgian architecture of colonial days. Built in 1765 and used during the American Revolution as George Washington's headquarters, the interior is now beautifully restored with period furniture, particularly French, that belonged to the Jumels or is associated with them.

Religion has always played an important part in the lives of black Americans. The Black Muslims have flourished in recent years, and some evangelical Protestant sects have transformed ancient movie houses into "pop" temples. To attend one of these services —choose one of the churches around Edgecombe Avenue— ask the minister if the congregation would object to your presence.

The east side of Harlem, largely the domain of Puerto Ricans, is called East or Spanish Harlem. Visit **El Museo del Barrio** (Fifth Avenue at East 104th Street), a museum devoted to the art and culture of Latin America.

MUSEUMS

The museums alone—there are more than 100 of them—qualify New York as one of the world's great cultural capitals.

At the Museum of Natural History it's not a question of burying your head in the sand.

Major Museums

American Museum of Natural History

Central Park West at West 79th Street. Open Mon., Tues., Thurs., Sun. 10 a.m.–5.45 p.m.; Wed., Fri., Sat. 10 a.m.–9 p.m.

This is the largest natural history museum in the world, and most of the rooms have remarkable displays. Be sure to see the section on minerals and precious stones, featuring the Star of India—the largest sapphire ever found—alongside moonstones and other gems.

Dinosaur exhibits fill two of the great halls. Also outstanding: some rooms devoted to Africa and South America. There's something here from every continent, covering the whole of the animal kingdom and a multitude of primitive civilizations.

In the museum's **Naturemax Theater**, a hall with a four-storey-high and 66-foot-wide screen, you can watch films on the wonders of the earth.

Next door is the **Hayden Planetarium**, known for its sparkling programmes about the stars and space exploration. The **Laserium** (same building) has

sound and light shows featuring the laser beam on Friday and Saturday evenings.

The Brooklyn Museum

Eastern Parkway at Washington Avenue (Brooklyn). Open Wed.–Sun. 10 a.m.–5 p.m.

Take the No. 2 or 3 express subway from Times Square. The trip to the nearest station (Eastern Parkway–Brooklyn Museum) takes half an hour.

The pre-Columbian art alone would make this an important museum. But the sections devoted to Egyptian, Far Eastern and Persian art are also exceptional. The costume museum is lovely, and the remaining rooms feature a permanent exhibition of American furniture from the time of the first settlers. The museum overlooks Prospect Park, where you can spend a pleasant afternoon if you're tired of the city.

Ellis Island Immigration Museum

See The Statue of Liberty and Ellis Island, pp. 73–76.

The Metropolitan Museum of Art

Fifth Avenue at East 82nd Street. Open Sun., Tues., Wed., Thurs. 9.30 a.m.–5.15 p.m.; Fri., Sat. 9.30 a.m.–8.45 p.m.

A world in itself, the "Met" has nearly 250 rooms; 4,500 paintings and drawings; a million prints; 4,000 musical instruments; and countless pieces of furniture and sculpture. Only a quarter of the collection is on display at any one time. You can't expect to see even a representative amount of the whole museum in one visit. Concentrate on one or two of the departments, and you'll come away enriched and not too exhausted.

You may like to start in the basement, where a shop sells posters of special exhibitions and reproductions. Also in the basement is the **Costume Institute**, showcasing the clothes of kings and queens, clowns and clergymen, monks and magicians, as well as exhibitions for children and special children's programmes on weekends.

As you enter the lobby on the main floor, you're likely to be impressed by the wonderful arrangements of fresh flowers—the legacy of a rich American who left her money to the museum for this purpose.

What makes the Metropolitan easier to "take" than many big museums is its ingenious display of exhibits in appropriate environments. Thus in the

Egyptian Department, north of the main floor lobby, you can enter a reconstructed mausoleum, mummies and all. Next to it, in a special wing, the **Temple of Dendur** was brought from the banks of the Nile to be reassembled here stone by stone. The temple was a gift from Egypt in gratitude for American help in saving the Abu Simbel Temple from the waters of the Aswan Dam.

Another striking setting, at the far west end of the main floor, is the **Lehman Collection**, which presents the donor's fine early Italian and French Impressionist paintings in the original, elegantly furnished decor of his home.

And the **Michael C. Rockefeller Wing** houses a superb collection of primitive art in a spacious, greenhouse-like hall.

The **American Wing**, practically a museum unto itself, is a glorious celebration of the architecture, decorative and fine arts of American life from the earliest colonial days to the present. You can climb the majestic wrought-iron and bronze staircase designed by Louis Sullivan for the late 19th-century Chicago Stock Exchange (now demolished) or a superbly carved wooden staircase from a simple New Hampshire house of 1700. One wall comprises the complete marble façade of the imposing 1824 U.S. Branch Bank brought from Wall Street.

Furniture is displayed in period rooms partially lit by Tiffany glass windows. People who tend to think of American painting only in avant-garde terms since World War II will be pleasantly surprised by the splendid canvases of Winslow Homer, the grand portraits by Whistler and Sargent, and the disturbing realism of Edward Hopper.

On the second floor, 35 rooms are devoted in more conventional style to **European painting** from the 15th century to the 20th. Some of the highlights: a pensive *Madonna and Child* by Bellini and a hilarious *Hunting Scene* by Piero de Cosimo. The masterpieces of the Dutch collection are Rembrandt's wistfully profound *Aristotle with the Bust of Homer* and Jan Vermeer's *Girl Asleep at a Table*. Of the French, Manet, Degas and Cézanne are the best of their 19th-century rooms. Velázquez and El Greco dominate the Spanish rooms, but the *Blind Man's Meal* by their compatriot, Picasso, is emotionally even more powerful. Turner dominates the British collection.

A delightful touch in the European collection, very characteristic of the Metropolitan's bold display technique, is Jean Dupas's lovely mural in glass, gold and silver leaf, rescued from the French *Normandie* ocean liner. The mural depicts the history of navigation.

And the museum continues to grow: the **20th-century wing**, nearly as big as the entire Museum of Modern Art, opened to acclaim in 1987. Featured here are paintings, sculpture and the decorative arts from Europe and America. In the 20th-century room, Americans Pollock, Kline and de Kooning shine.

The Museum of Modern Art

West 53rd Street between Fifth and Sixth avenues. Open Fri.–Tues. 11 a.m.–6 p.m.; Thurs. 11 a.m.–9 p.m.

Designed by Philip Goodwin and Edward Durell Stone, with additions by Philip Johnson and Cesar Pelli, the MOMA, as it's affectionately known, is devoted to works of art from 1880 to the present day. The museum has more than 70,000 works, but only a portion of the collection is on view at any one time.

Go into the garden—in summer it's a cool haven as well as the setting for sculptures by Renoir, Rodin, Maillol, Picasso, Moore and Calder. From here, glass-enclosed escalators lead into the modernized MOMA. (Sale of air rights to

New York's oldest "skyscraper" can be seen at the Met.

the property helped to pay for the face-lift. Now a residential skyscraper called Museum Tower soars high above West 53rd Street.)

Temporary exhibitions and recent acquisitions appear on the ground floor of the west wing. But why not begin at the beginning, with the forerunners of contemporary art? The display may vary, but you will certainly find canvases by artists representing all major modern movements, from Impressionists to Futurists.

There are masterpieces galore in the galleries of the MOMA: from Monet's exquisite *Water Lilies,* Picasso's ironic and tender *Les Demoiselles d'Avignon* and Piet Mondrian's dynamic *Broadway Boogie Woogie* to the perverse

Persistence of Memory by Dali, the haunting *Target with Four Faces* by Johns and Andrew Wyeth's American icon, *Christina's World.*

MOMA lays claim to some great pieces of sculpture, notably Alberto Giacometti's *The Palace at 4 a.m.* and a Duchamp "ready-made", the *Bicycle Wheel.* There's a prodigious photography collection and a section devoted to architecture and design. Here you'll see a Wedgwood cup and saucer from 1768, and a Bang & Olufsen "Beogram 4002" turntable designed by Jakob Jensen—an object as modern as MOMA itself.

Every day the museum screens several films from the history of cinema. No additional admission is charged.

THE NEW YORK SCHOOL

New York was a provincial backwater when émigré artists from Europe arrived on the scene shortly before World War II. Members of the avant-garde, they made an immediate impact on the cultural life of the city, fostering the development of America's first truly innovative school of painting, the New York school of abstract expressionists.

The key figure was Jackson Pollock, from Wyoming, who pioneered the technique of action painting. He applied colour to the canvas in a series of splashes and dribbles, leaving composition to chance. Dutch-born Willem de Kooning followed suit, though sometimes a recognizable subject emerges in his work. Another leading member of the school was Pennsylvanian Franz Kline, famous for his abstract canvases in black, white and grey.

Whitney Museum of American Art

Madison Avenue at East 75th Street. Open Tues. 1–8 p.m.; Wed.–Sat. 11 a.m.–5 p.m.; Sun. noon–6 p.m. Admission free on Tuesday evenings.

The Whitney, devoted to 20th-century American art, concentrates on the works of living artists in both permanent and changing exhibitions. Also included are contemporary film and video productions. Museum branches are located at Equitable Center, Seventh Avenue between West 51st and 52nd streets (works from the permanent collection and changing exhibitions in two

"Public relations" outside the Museum of Modern Art.

separate galleries), at Philip Morris, Park Avenue at East 42nd Street (a sculpture court and gallery), and downtown at Federal Reserve Plaza, Maiden Lane at Nassau Street (changing exhibitions on all the visual arts).

Other Art and History Museums

American Craft Museum

In the E.F. Hutton tower on West 53rd Street, across from the Museum of Modern Art. Open Tues. 10 a.m.–8 p.m.; Wed.–Sun. 10 a.m.–5 p.m.

Consider the relationship between function and decoration as you look over the best in American crafts, from old-fashioned rockers to seatless chairs.

The Cloisters

Fort Tryon Park. (This is a branch of the Metropolitan Museum of Art.) Open Tues.–Sun. 9.30 a.m.–4.45 p.m.; March–Oct. Tues.–Sun. 9.30 a.m.–5.15 p.m.

We have to thank a millionaire, John D. Rockefeller, Jr., for this strange concoction of medieval ruins, brought from France, Italy and Spain, reassembled as a fortified monastery.

There are some lovely things here, including the chapel of San Martín de Fuentidueña from Segovia, the Romanesque cloister of St. Michel-de-Cuxa from the Pyrenees, the cathedral treasury, the Unicorn and Burgos tapestries and the famous Mérode triptych. The garden is fragrant with medicinal herbs used in the Middle Ages.

Cooper-Hewitt Museum

East 91st Street at Fifth Avenue. Open Tues. 10 a.m.–9 p.m.; Wed.–Sat. 10 a.m.–5 p.m.; Sun. noon–5 p.m.

Located in the sumptuous mansion built for Andrew Carnegie in 1900, it owns one of the largest collections of decorative art in the U.S.

The Frick Collection

East 70th Street at Fifth Avenue. Open Tues.–Sat. 10 a.m.–6 p.m.; Sun. 1–6 p.m. Children from 10 to 16 admitted if accompanied by an adult, no children under 10.

Henry Clay Frick, of Swiss origin, was a steel magnate who, like other American multimillionaires of the early 20th century, set aside part of his fortune for acquiring works of art. The museum used to be his home, so you can get some idea of the way rich New Yorkers used to live.

There is an 18th-century French boudoir with eight panels commissioned from François Boucher by Madame de Pompadour, a Fragonard salon containing an assortment of fine pieces and a dining room with portraits by Hogarth, Reynolds and Gainsborough. Other treasures include El Greco's *St. Jerome as Cardinal,* Holbein portraits, *Philip of Spain* by Velázquez, *Education of the Virgin* by de La Tour, Dutch landscapes, some striking full-length portraits by James Whistler and three Rembrandts. The carpets, furniture and exhibits are all priceless. You can attend chamber music concerts on Sundays in winter; write in advance for free tickets. The concerts are held in one of the most charming areas of the museum, the glass-domed, marble-floored courtyard with its pool and fountain.

Solomon R. Guggenheim Museum

Fifth Avenue at East 89th Street. Open Tues. 11 a.m.–8 p.m.; Wed.–Sun. 11 a.m.–5 p.m.

The building, by Frank Lloyd Wright, is a worthy attraction in itself. Some call it a giant snail, others proclaim it a masterpiece of New York architecture. Wright himself regarded it as a piece of sculpture. Inside, a wide spiral ramp—the gallery—runs around the wall. The sky-lit core is empty. The incline, the colour of the wall and the lighting have all been selected carefully so as not to tire the viewer's eyes.

The basic collection is that of Solomon R. Guggenheim, who came here from Switzerland and made his fortune in copper. His collection has since been enlarged to include works by Kandinsky, Klee and Chagall, plus thousands of others. The Justin K. Thannhauser collection, housed in an annexe, contains paintings by Renoir, Monet, Cézanne, van Gogh, Gauguin and Degas. The museum holds eight to a dozen different exhibitions each year.

International Center of Photography

Fifth Avenue at East 94th Street. Open Tues. noon–8 p.m.; Wed.–Fri. noon–5 p.m.; Sat., Sun. 11 a.m.–6 p.m. Midtown branch at Avenue of the Americas and West 43rd Street: Tues., Wed., Fri.–Sun. 11 a.m.–6 p.m.; Thurs. 11 a.m.–8 p.m.

Library, exhibition galleries and laboratories.

The New-York Historical Society

Central Park West at West 77th Street. Open Tues.–Sun. 10 a.m.–5 p.m.

Important museum and research library for American history.

Science and Theme Museums

The American Museum of the Moving Image, 35th Avenue at 36th Street (Astoria, Queens). Open Tues.–Fri. noon–4 p.m.; Sat., Sun. noon–6 p.m. Dedicated to the history of the motion picture with hands-on displays, original movie sets, costumes and two screening theatres.

IBM Gallery of Science and Art, Madison Avenue between East 56th and 57th streets. Open Tues.–Sat. 11 a.m.–6 p.m. Host of changing exhibitions giving exposure to art originating in lesser known regions of the U.S. and those countries where IBM operates.

Intrepid Sea-Air-Space Museum, Pier 86, West 46th Street at Twelfth Avenue. Open Wed.–Sun. 10 a.m.–5 p.m. World War II-era aircraft carrier. Extensive exhibits and audio-visual presentations.

Museum of the City of New York, Fifth Avenue at East 103rd Street. Open Wed.–Sat. 10 a.m.–5 p.m.; Sun. 1–5 p.m. (See For Children, p. 90.)

Museum of Holography, Mercer Street at Canal Street (SoHo). Open Tues.–Sun. 11 a.m.–6 p.m. A small museum devoted to the art of the hologram (pictures developed by laser light creating three-dimensional images).

National Museum of the American Indian, Smithsonian Institution, Audubon Terrace at Broadway and West 155th Street. Open Tues.–Sat. 10 a.m.–5 p.m.; Sun. 1–5 p.m. The world's largest collection of Indian art and artefacts of North, Central and South America.

Pierpont Morgan Library, East 36th Street at Madison Avenue. Open Tues.–Sat. 10.30 a.m.–5 p.m.; Sun. 1–5 p.m. Rare books, illuminated manuscripts, Old Master paintings, Florentine sculpture, etc., amassed by the American tycoon, J. Pierpont Morgan.

South Street Seaport Museum, East River at the foot of Fulton Street. Open weekdays 10 a.m.–5 p.m.; Sat., Sun. 10 a.m.–6 p.m. Restored seaport area of 19th-century buildings and sailing ships (see p. 43).

EXCURSIONS

The Statue of Liberty and Ellis Island

For millions of immigrants the **Statue of Liberty**, or more simply "the Lady", was their first glimpse of America, a symbol of the New World.

The statue, some ten years in the building, was a gift from France to the United States in recognition of the friendship between the two countries, and was to serve as a beacon for those arriving in the New World from the Old.

Frédéric-Auguste Bartholdi's 151-foot-high structure was one of those wild dreams that become reality. Engineering expertise had to be harnessed to art, so Bartholdi called in Gustave Eiffel—of Eiffel Tower fame—to help translate his artistic vision into metal. Skilled workmen in Paris erected the statue in 1884, as scores of Parisians watched her crowned head rise above their rooftops. It was later dismantled and shipped over in 214 huge wooden crates for reassembly on Liberty Island.

The Statue of "Liberty Enlightening the World" was officially unveiled by President Cleveland on October 28, 1886.

The ferry to the statue on Liberty Island leaves from Battery Park on the southern tip of Manhattan; tickets are available at Castle Clinton. Try to make the trip in the morning (ferry: daily every 45 minutes from 9.30 a.m.–3.30 p.m.; sights: open daily 9 a.m.–5 p.m.), and allow at least two hours' sightseeing on each island. The crossing to Liberty Island takes about 15 minutes. After your visit here, you can reboard the ferry for the trip to Ellis Island.

Once on Liberty Island, most visitors head for the elevator that services the promenade at the top of the 89-foot base of the statue (elevator queues are commonly two to three hours long), from where there are spectacular **views** of the Manhattan skyline. To reach the lady's crown, you have to climb a 22-storey staircase from the foot of the statue. The statue's base houses the **American Museum of Immigration**, featuring early immigrant photos and personal belongings.

Thanks to an extensive restoration programme, the **Ellis Island Immigration Museum** on the islet just north of the Statue of Liberty opened its doors in 1990. It retraces, through a touching

introductory film, audio-visual displays and permanent and changing exhibitions, the sufferings and joys of some 16 million immigrants. During the island's peak immigration years (1892–1924), over 12 million people went through screening here.

Each day the transatlantic steamers would anchor at Quarantine in the New York Narrows. By barges, the human cargoes would be shunted to Ellis Island where, after leaving their worldly belongings below, they would troop up flights of stairs to the Great Hall to undergo medical scrutiny. Then, through interpreters, they would face a barrage of questions. Their whole future, hopes and dreams depended on making it through this examination—a human drama re-enacted millions of times. Before Americans set up consular missions abroad, there was no preliminary selection: an official in a bad mood, an overconscientious doctor, or an eye infection contracted on the voyage might cause the hopeful immigrant to be rejected.

Pages 74–75: What monument in the world is more charged with meaning?

In fact, 80 per cent of those that came "passed" unencumbered within three to five hours; 20 per cent were detained and, of them, only 2 per cent—or 250,000 people in all—were actually refused entry.

Boat and Helicopter Excursions

Your visit to New York would not be complete without the traditional **boat ride around Manhattan**. The Circle Line offers the classic trip leaving from Pier 83 on the Hudson River at West 43rd Street (see Boat Excursions, p. 103). You may want to combine this outing with a visit to the museum-ship *Intrepid,* docked at Pier 86 (see p. 72).

The boat goes round the island of Manhattan, a 35-mile voyage that takes three hours. A guide indicates points of interest: architectural, historic, cultural or just anecdotal. If you can't spare three hours, board the Seaport Line's replica paddleboat for a 90-minute cruise around lower Manhattan—or take the **ferry to Staten Island** from Battery Park for the cheapest tour in town.

Flying over the skyscraper skyline in a **helicopter** is an unforgettable experience. Various

NEW YORK'S BEST BRIDGES

Water-laced New York has 65 bridges to hold it together, 14 that connect the isle of Manhattan with the surrounding area.

The 1,595-foot **Brooklyn Bridge** created a sensation when it opened in 1883. But it was plagued by misfortune from the start. Its engineer, John Roebling, died in the early phases of the project as a result of an accident, and his son, who carried on the work, was paralyzed by the "bends" suffered in the course of the job. And they were not the only casualties. Nonetheless, the bridge, with its wire webbing, is a beautiful success and a favourite subject for photographers and Sunday painters. The view from the bridge is best at night.

The double-decker **George Washington Bridge** spans the Hudson between Manhattan and New Jersey. Designed by O.H. Ammann, its graceful lines show up best at night when the bridge is illuminated.

Newest on the New York horizon is one of the world's longest suspension structures (4,260 feet), the **Verrazano-Narrows Bridge** from Brooklyn to Staten Island, which is also the work of Ammann. It's named after the Italian who discovered New York Bay in 1524, landing near the bridge's Staten Island base.

tours are available. The shortest flight lasts only five minutes and doesn't go beyond the United Nations area. The longest covers the whole town. It's probably best to take a tour covering the United Nations, World Trade Center, midtown Manhattan and Central Park. There are departures throughout the day. You may have to wait a while around midday at peak tourist season. Flights leave either from the East River at East 34th Street (Island Helicopter) or from the Heliport at the foot of West 30th Street on the Hudson River (Liberty Helicopter Tours).

For a slightly lower bird's-eye view, try the aerial tramway connecting Manhattan and Roosevelt Island. It leaves from Second Avenue at East 60th Street.

Brooklyn Heights

Why not go beyond Manhattan at least once for a visit to Brooklyn? With its 2¼ million inhabitants, it has a greater population than Manhattan and, indeed, is one of the largest urban centres in America. Brooklynites have a strong pride in their accent and their traditions, and they don't cross over to Manhattan unless they really have to.

Brooklyn Heights, on the East River, is one of the prettiest neighbourhoods. To get there, take the subway (No. 2 or 3) as far as the Clark Street Station. You'll come out in the basement of what used to be the St. George Hotel, once among the grandest in New York.

Outside, turn west along Clark Street. After three blocks you'll come to the **Promenade**, an esplanade with one of the most impressive **views** in the world: at your feet are ships unloading their cargoes of sugar and coffee; in front of you is downtown Manhattan with all its bridges; beyond that, the Bay of New York and the Statue of Liberty. In the late afternoon, when the sun is setting, the sight will take your breath away.

At the end of the Promenade, walk south along **Hicks Street**, a shady street in a quarter that has barely changed since 1860. The brownstones—little red-brick houses—are still in fashion and prices here are rocketing. When you reach **Atlantic Avenue**, one of the longest streets in Brooklyn, it's like stepping into another world—of Arab restaurants and grocers' stores. Here you can eat very good Egyptian and Lebanese food at prices well below those in Manhattan. On Sundays Atlantic Avenue positively bustles with Americans of Middle Eastern descent who come to do their shopping.

Bronx Park

Other good reasons for venturing beyond the confines of Manhattan are the **Bronx Zoo** (open weekdays 10 a.m.–5 p.m.; Sat., Sun. 10 a.m.–5.30 p.m.; Nov.–Feb. daily 10 a.m.–4.30 p.m.)—largest in the United States—and the sparkling **New York Botanical Garden Conservatory** (open Tues.–Sun. 10 a.m.–5 p.m.; in winter Tues.–Sun. 10 a.m.–4 p.m.). Both are located in Bronx Park. The all-glass conservatory, with a 90-foot-high crystal dome, covers almost an acre. Inside, you will find orchids and palm trees, a gurgling waterfall and the lush aroma of citrus trees. Take the D or No. 4 train to Bedford Park Boulevard and walk east. For the zoo, get off at Pelham Parkway on the No. 2 express subway and walk west to the Bronxdale entrance.

In New York you can set your own pace, but New Yorkers don't like to be caught doing only one thing at a time.

HEIGHTS COTTAGE

WHAT TO DO

SHOPPING

One of the great joys of New York is window shopping. Just stroll down Fifth Avenue from 59th Street, preferably on a sunny day. You can't help being dazzled by the fabulous jewellery displays, luxurious leather goods, exquisite crystal and porcelain, discount stores and, of course, clothes, clothes, clothes.

There's always some kind of sale going on in New York. The Sunday papers are full of advertisements on current ones, as well as ads of discount stores specializing in electronic equipment.

What to Buy

Arts and antiques. Art galleries and antique shops are found throughout the city, with items that range from the exorbitant to the relatively affordable. The largest concentration of galleries is situated along East 57th Street and in SoHo. Two institutions worth visiting for their breathtaking choice: the Manhattan Art & Antiques Center (Second Avenue between East 55th and 56th streets), boasting more than a hundred shops and galleries, and the Place des Antiquaires (East 57th Street between Park and Lexington avenues), with 50-odd shops.

Reflecting on the shopping possibilities in New York.

Cameras, calculators, radios, etc. Most of the products are Japanese. The price tags reflect cut-rate practices.

Clothing. The prodigious array of ready-to-wear clothes will impress all but the most hardened shopper. The designs of French and American couturiers hang side by side in the high-fashion boutiques. And next door you'll find copies produced for less affluent customers.

Cosmetics. Shop around the department stores for special bonus offers on your favourite beauty products. Promotion campaigns by the leading firms, featuring free samples, make the tour of the town.

Gadgets. In this paradise for gadget-lovers, you can certainly find an original gift to take home. The best selection appears just before Christmas in speciality shops and the household departments of big stores. Hammacher Schlemmer (147 East 57th Street) takes the prize in this category.

Jewellery. Ranging from mass-produced costume jewellery in the very latest styles to the most incredibly elaborate, expensive and original creations, not forgetting the budget-wise diamond centre on West 47th Street and handmade items, mostly in silver and copper, in Greenwich Village boutiques.

Records and books. Choose from a vast selection of the latest releases in classical, rock, folk, jazz and pop music. Tower Records and Sam Goody's are the places to go. In the book realm, the real bargains are items that have been on the shelves for a few years—art books and publications on specialized or offbeat subjects. Barnes & Noble Bookstore (Fifth Avenue at East 18th Street), one of the world's largest bookshops, has several midtown branches. Other fine bookstores include Doubleday Book Shop (largest branch at Fifth Avenue and West 57th Street), Rizzoli (31 West 57th Street) and Strand Book Store (Broadway at East 12th Street).

Sports equipment. Again, a wide choice, expert advice and discount possibilities in tennis racquets, golf clubs and skis.

Toys. Some brands have a justly deserved reputation for durability. Educational toys abound but you can still find things that are just plain fun. The ultimate toy store is F.A.O. Schwarz (Fifth Avenue at East 58th Street), where you can consider buying a doll's house for $10,000.

When and Where to Shop

As a general rule, stores are open Monday to Saturday from 10 a.m. to 6 p.m. Many shops and department stores open at least one night a week, usually Thursdays. All the large department stores are open Sunday afternoons. Generally, shops in Greenwich Village, SoHo and Chelsea (shopping concentrated on Seventh Avenue from West 14th to 23rd streets) are open from noon to 7 or 8 p.m., except Mondays.

In small shops with "Going out of business" signs in the window, selling cameras, Irish linen, electronic watches and radios, goods tend to be unreliable and overpriced. Snub anyone who tries to sell you anything on the street.

Department stores exist in many shapes and sizes. Bloomingdale's (Third Avenue at East 59th Street) is almost a city in itself. A store you absolutely must visit for the most up-to-the-minute clothing, furniture (see their model rooms), accessories and fine gourmet shop. In fact, just about everything. Macy's (West 34th Street at Broadway), known as the world's largest department store, does sell everything!

For fine fashions, saunter down Fifth Avenue from 58th to 39th streets stopping at Bergdorf Goodman, Henri Bendel, Bonwit Teller, Saks Fifth Avenue and Lord & Taylor. On Seventh Avenue at West 17th Street, Barneys New York concentrates on exclusive designer clothes for men and women and features individual departments for special sizes. For budget-minded shoppers, Alexander's (Lexington Avenue at East 58th Street) offers fashion and gadgets at competitive prices.

Malls and centres. Some of the city's most prestigious shops occupy premises in Trump Tower (Fifth Avenue at East 56th Street), next door to Tiffany's. The building is linked to Bonwit Teller and the IBM Building via a spacious passageway complete with internal waterfall. Further down Fifth Avenue, more than 200 stores fill the underground and street-level shopping complex of Rockefeller Center. At Fifth Avenue and East 47th Street, the fashionable four-level 575 Fifth Avenue mall is crowned by a stained-glass ceiling. The Market at Citicorp Center (see p. 30) features three floors of bright and varied shops while the stores of the A & S Plaza (Avenue of the Americas between West 32nd and 33rd streets) are distributed on eight floors. In downtown Manhattan the SoHo Emporium (West Broadway between Spring and Broome streets) houses some 40 chic shops under a Civil War-period roof, and in the Financial District the myriad stores and boutiques in the World Trade Center and the World Financial Center cater for a multitude of tastes.

ENTERTAINMENT

When the sun goes down and the theatre marquees light up, New York starts moving to another rhythm. A quick tour of the city's nightlife might include some of the following: a brash, exuberant Broadway musical; a dim, smoke-filled room throbbing to a saxophone's wail; block-long queues waiting patiently to see a film; elegant champagne-sipping first-nighters at the Met; a tinkling piano playing Gershwin at a 40s-style bar; and, inevitably, the cool frenzy of the disco dancers. And you haven't even begun to cover the scene. To find out what's on, consult the Friday newspapers, the "Arts & Leisure" section of the Sunday *New York Times* or the weekly

publications *New York* and *The Village Voice*. For details on obtaining theatre and concert tickets, see p. 119.

Theatre

One of the main reasons for visiting New York is to take in a few shows. Broadway means musicals, comedies and conventional drama. (But most of the theatres are physically off Broadway, clustered around the side streets from West 44th to 50th streets.) Broadway has the big stars and the elaborate productions. Tickets for hit shows

No sign of an energy crisis here—Lincoln Center by night.

can be very difficult to obtain at short notice, so it's best to write ahead if you have your heart set on a particular one. Curtain-up time is usually 8 p.m., with matinées on Wednesdays, Saturdays and sometimes Sundays.

Off-Broadway and Off-Off-Broadway theatres are scattered all over town. Generally smaller, they can be top-flight or strictly amateur affairs. But the tickets are invariably cheaper. The plays range from revivals of the classics to the most avant-garde theatrical experiments. The Public Theater (425 Lafayette Street), which may have several different productions going at once, can usually be counted on for an interesting evening.

Dance

When it comes to dance, New York fairly bubbles over with activity. This is the headquarters of modern dance, and classical ballet makes a creditable showing, too. Between the resident companies—New York City Ballet, Joffrey Ballet, Merce Cunningham, Alvin Ailey, Dance Theatre of Harlem and the American Ballet Theatre—and up-and-coming groups like Plath/Taucher, dance fans are really spoiled for choice.

Opera and Concert

The city's two major opera companies occupy adjoining buildings in Lincoln Center. The Met may have the glamour and the Italian tenors but the New York City Opera can lay claim to a more modern and adventurous repertory. Both are superb. As for concerts of classical music, you're likely to find 30 or so scheduled for a single evening—with the New York Philharmonic (also at Lincoln Center) heading the bill. Carnegie Hall, known for its excellent acoustics, plays host to outstanding visiting artists. Free concerts are held frequently in the Bruno Walter Auditorium of the New York Public Library at Lincoln Center. Summers, the Met and the Philharmonic give free performances in the city's parks.

Cinemas

Every New York neighbourhood has its movie theatres, but the two largest concentrations are in the Times Square area and along Third Avenue above East 57th Street. These feature the newest films and the highest prices. Certain cinemas specialize in reruns of old Hollywood classics and subtitled foreign films, and several museums and societies have cinema halls which put on special-interest programmes. Queuing up outside the theatre can be fun, too—unless, of course, the weather is really miserable.

The Late-Night Scene

Great jazz clubs, featuring everything from modern and avant-garde to traditional jazz, are spread all over the city, but the largest concentration is to be found in the Village and SoHo. A special number, Jazzline 1-718-465-7500, gives details about who's playing where.

Shows are presented nightly at most of New York's comedy clubs, some of which have been the launching stage for the nation's top comedians. Other nightlife attractions: rock, pop and dance (or "ballroom") clubs—including some fancy discos—and hilarious cabaret shows.

Yes, you can still find old-fashioned nightclubs and supper clubs in New York. You can dance to sweet music and be entertained in a brassy or silky style. Be prepared to spend. Ethnic nightclubs—Spanish, Mexican, Brazilian, French, Italian—vary the scene.

SPORTS

As unlikely as it may seem, many of those sedentary-looking New Yorkers are active sportsmen, and they have more facilities at their disposal than most other city-dwellers.

In Central Park you can hire a bicycle or a boat. To play tennis there, you'll need a permit for the season (not required for lessons), but there are courts elsewhere in the city (see the Yellow Pages of the telephone directory) for hire by the hour. Otherwise, you can just follow the example of the thousands of New Yorkers who jog in Central Park and along the city pavements. In winter there's ice skating in the park and at Rockefeller Center.

New York boasts 18 miles of public beaches with reasonably clean—if sometimes chilly—water. However, fear of stumbling on syringes left in the sand by drug addicts keeps wary citizens away.

Armchair sportsmen will find plenty to follow on television. The American networks provide excellent coverage of sporting events.

The baseball season runs from April to late September; football (American-style) from September to late December. If

BALL
STRIKE
OUT
CIN
NY
3RD INN
Armitron
AMERICA'S WATCH
AB 44
AVG .234
338

you want to attend a big game, buy your ticket in advance. Ask at the hotel desk or go to a Ticketron (tel. 399-4444) outlet. For less important games, you can probably get tickets at the gate. Consult the Friday newspapers for a rundown on the weekend sports activities.

The Mets baseball team plays at Shea Stadium in Queens, not far from LaGuardia Airport. The No. 7 (Flushing) subway, from Grand Central, stops right at the stadium.

The Yankees (baseball) can be seen at Yankee Stadium in the Bronx (East 161st Street and River Avenue), reached on the No. 4 or D subway. The Giants and Jets (football) are based at the Meadowlands (Giants Stadium) in northern New Jersey, a vast sports and entertainment complex that also houses the New Jersey Nets (basketball) and Devils (ice hockey). Harness, thoroughbred and motor racing events also bring the fans out to the Meadowlands.

The important basketball (New York Knicks) and ice-hockey (New York Rangers) teams play at Madison Square Garden. The Garden is also the place to see world championship boxing, horse shows and various other sporting events. You may be able to get tickets for individual matches at the Garden's box office.

New Yorkers love to bet on horses. The two big race tracks are Aqueduct (Queens) and Belmont (Long Island). The trotters go through their paces at Roosevelt Raceway on Long Island, the Meadowlands and at Yonkers Raceway. Also on Long Island is the Nassau Coliseum, home to New York's ice-hockey team, the Islanders.

Among classic sports fixtures, the U.S. Open Tennis Championships take place at Flushing Meadows in Queens in August/September. In late October/early November, some 25,000 sprinters participate in the 26 1/5-mile New York City Marathon, which starts on Staten Island and ends in Central Park.

In spite of all the competition of New York's theatres and clubs, baseball still manages to draw a full house.

FOR CHILDREN

Small children can scamper around in **Central Park**'s well-equipped adventure playgrounds. The Victorian **Belvedere Castle** (79th Street, south of the Great Lawn) has a Discovery Chamber and offers events for children of all ages. In the south-east corner of the park, visit the **Children's Zoo**.

At the **Children's Museum of Manhattan** (West 83rd Street between Broadway and Amsterdam Avenue)—with workshops for specific age groups, special events and exhibitions—kids can walk around on their own.

Most children absolutely adore the **American Museum of Natural History** (see pp. 62–64) with its skeletons of dinosaurs and stuffed animals displayed in their natural habitats. **Hayden Planetarium** next door puts on a super star show for older kids.

The **Museum of the City of New York** (see p. 72) has some wonderful old toys as well as marine and fire galleries.

Another option for a rainy day is the **National Museum of the American Indian, Smithsonian Institution** (see p. 72), a treasure house of "genuine" possessions of Sitting Bull and other Western heroes.

A trip to New York for any youngster would be incomplete without a visit to the city's most famous toy emporium, **F.A.O. Schwarz** (see p. 82). And, of course, many tourist attractions—like the boat trips (see p. 76), skyscraper peaks and the **South Street Seaport**—appeal to all age groups.

Outside Manhattan there's the mammoth **Bronx Zoo** (see p. 78) and the **New York Aquarium** on Coney Island in Brooklyn (West 8th Street at Surf Avenue; take the D or F express subway trains to West 8th Street Station–New York Aquarium). The aquarium features whales, sharks, dolphins and some 20,000 other creatures.

New York's own **Big Apple Circus** performs at different places during the year. And if you're going to be in town in the spring, you shouldn't miss the "Greatest Show on Earth", **Ringling Brothers Barnum & Bailey Circus**.

Central Park re-creates Wonderland for Mad Hatter kids.

EATING OUT

Parisian cuisine may be more refined, but New York's is incomparably more cosmopolitan. You have your pick of cooking from every corner of the globe—to say nothing of all-American steaks, hamburgers and first-class seafood.

Eating Habits

New Yorkers, resident and transient, seem to operate on staggered schedules. The late riser, finishing breakfast, may have to cede to the early lunchers. You'll see people eating in restaurants almost any time of day—when they're not snacking somewhere else.

Breakfast, served between 7 and 11 a.m., can consist of fruit juice, toast or Danish pastry (sweet roll) with coffee or tea (Continental breakfast) or the whole works: eggs (served with buttered toast and jam), sausages, pancakes (thick ones coated with maple syrup) or waffles in assorted flavours. British visitors may find American coffee a bit weak and may also be surprised to receive a second cup without asking.

New Yorkers have a snack... any time, any place, anywhere.

Brunch is a hybrid of breakfast and lunch, traditionally eaten on lazy Sundays any time between 11 a.m. and 3 p.m.

Lunch, from 11 a.m. to 2.30 p.m., is usually a hamburger or sandwich washed down with an icy Coke, iced tea in summer, a glass of iced water or coffee.

Dinner, from as early as 5.30 until 10.30 p.m., is often preceded and accompanied by cocktails.

Where to Eat

It all depends whether you crave *linguini* with clam sauce, stuffed cabbage, *canard à l'orange, Sauerbraten* with potato pancakes, *dim sum, paella, tempura, tacos* or just "two eggs over easy". You can find it all in New York. If you like hot and spicy food, look for snacks, appetizers (starters) or entrées (main courses) marked "Cajun style". A legacy of the 18th-century French-speaking immigrants to the U.S. from Canada's Acadia, Cajun dishes are now found on restaurant menus throughout the city.

Most parts of Manhattan are supplied with excellent restaurants. In the midtown area the best selection is in and around the Theater District between West 42nd and 55th streets and on the East Side between Madison and Second avenues. Further south, head for the Village, SoHo or one of the neighbourhoods of lower Manhattan—TriBeCa, Little Italy, Chinatown—or try South Street Seaport, the World Financial Center or the World Trade Center.

Coffee shops and self-service cafeterias, found all over town, offer hamburgers, French fries (chips), simple dishes and pastries. No alcohol is sold.

Delicatessens (delis), a cross between grocery stores and restaurants, are known for their gargantuan sandwiches with all kinds of bread, garnished with huge half-sour (cucumber) or dill pickles; other specialities include salads and hearty soups like mushroom-barley or refreshing cold borsch. Some delicatessens are kosher.

Ethnic restaurants, a term covering all foreign restaurants—Greek, Italian, Japanese, Chinese, Spanish, Mexican, Indian, Middle Eastern, German, Russian, Scandinavian and so on. There's something for every imaginable taste.

Some of the best Chinese and Italian restaurants are located in Chinatown and Little Italy. If German food takes your fancy, head up to East 86th Street in Yorkville between Lexington and First avenues. Middle Eastern restaurants can be found on Atlantic Avenue in Brooklyn or—along with Greek, French, Spanish and Filipino cuisine—on Eighth Avenue between West 37th and 53rd streets.

Fast-food chains. You'll see plenty of reminders that you're in the homeland of McDonald's, Kentucky Fried Chicken and followers.

Pizzerias serve a great variety of enormous pizzas, usually big enough for three people. But you can also buy pizza by the slice.

Sidewalk cafés have become very popular in recent years. They serve full meals, as well as *quiches, crêpes* and sandwiches. Some of the most pleasant are protected from the elements in the pedestrian areas, or atriums, of skyscrapers like the Trump Tower.

Take-outs are small kitchens where you can order a meal, sandwich, salads, assorted groceries and soft drinks to take out and eat elsewhere.

What to Eat

Sandwiches start with white, rye, pumpernickel or whole-wheat bread, a roll, bagel (doughnut-shaped roll) or pitta, Arab flat bread. Classic fillings include chicken, tuna and egg salads; lox (smoked salmon) with cream cheese, a delicious Jewish speciality served on a bagel; and chopped liver or pastrami (seasoned smoked beef), also of Jewish descent. There are also club sandwiches—three slices of toast interspersed with lettuce, tomato, bacon and sometimes cheese; the hot dog, a New York invention usually served with sauerkraut or fried onions and mustard; and hamburgers, the "national dish", generally much bigger and better than their British equivalents.

Soups. Many Americans often lunch on soup rather than a hamburger, and more and more small restaurants include a variety of soups on their menu. Vichyssoise (don't let the name mislead you, it's an American recipe) is in fact a chilled concoction of leeks, potatoes and onions; chilli con carne, often served as a soup, is a substantial and spicy stew of kidney beans, ground beef, onions and tomatoes.

Salads. Many restaurants feature an appetizing self-service salad bar. When ordering a salad you'll be asked what kind of dressing you prefer: French (creamy, with tomato flavour), Russian (mayonnaise and chilli sauce), Italian (oil, vinegar, garlic and herbs), Roquefort or blue cheese. You can always ask for plain oil and vinegar.

The "chef's salad", which may include ham, cheese and chicken, is a meal in itself; raw spinach salad with mushrooms ranks as a great American original; Caesar salad has romaine lettuce and a raw egg in the dressing; coleslaw (cabbage salad) often appears with sandwiches; Waldorf salad is composed of apples, walnuts and mayonnaise. You'll also find a wide variety of vegetable and fruit salads—often with cottage cheese—specially conceived for weight watchers.

Meat. Beef takes first place. It comes in enormous portions and is almost invariably tender. In steakhouses you often pay a flat rate for a steak, a baked potato with sour cream or French fries (chips), a self-service salad bar, and, in some cases, as much wine, beer or sangria as you like.

"Spare ribs" are pork ribs, marinated in a spicy sauce, baked or grilled and eaten with your fingers. Ham steak with a slice of pineapple is a speciality from the South. Long Island ducklings are famous for their flavour. Finally, stuffed turkey, the all-American holiday favourite, appears on menus all year round.

Fish and seafood. It's too often forgotten that New York is an ocean port abounding with fresh seafood. If you like shellfish, make the most of your stay here. The Long Island Blue Point oysters, subject to strict inspection, are a real delicacy.

Oysters and clams on the half-shell come with chilli and horseradish sauces and small crackers (biscuits). "Oysters Rockefeller", covered with spinach, sprinkled with bread-crumbs and then browned under a grill, are an unexpected but successful combination.

For a change from the perennial shrimp (prawn) cocktail, try soft-shell crabs (in spring and summer). You can eat almost every morsel of these crabs, caught after they've cast their shells.

Scallops, lobster and Nova Scotia salmon are special treats and much cheaper than their European counterparts.

Fish is good, too, usually grilled or deep-fried in batter. Some superstition prompts Americans to serve them with head and tail chopped off.

Cheese. It's unusual to find a cheese board served except in New York's French restaurants. Cheese is imported from all over Europe. In addition, the U.S. produces its own British-, Dutch- and Swiss-style cheeses, of which the sharper ones approach their European equivalents. The best of the locally made French cheeses are the creamy versions spiced with herbs and garlic.

Desserts. Ice cream comes in a wonderful variety of flavours. Pastries and pies are not always as good, though there are exceptions—especially cheesecake and apple pie, topped with a scoop of ice cream *(à la mode)* or whipped cream, and pumpkin pie, a Thanksgiving Day tradition. Rice pudding and jello (jelly) are coffee-shop staples.

In most restaurants you can

ask for fresh fruit or a fruit salad, which is sometimes offered as a first course.

Drinks. You'll be given a glass of iced water at the start of your meal if you ask for one. Iced tea is a standby in the warmer months. Many Americans drink coffee with their meal.

Soft drinks are very popular, with cola drinks leading the market. You can always get one that is artificially sweetened.

Beer, served ice cold, falls into the lager category. You can often find pale or brown ale and many foreign beers, either imported or manufactured under licence.

New York produces some decent wines; those from California are even better, especially the white ones. You can order domestic wine by the bottle or, in many places, by the glass or carafe as the "house wine". French and Italian wines, at reasonable prices, also appear on menus.

Since Americans discovered wine, spirits have gone somewhat out of fashion. But not the cocktail hour! Dry martinis (gin and a few drops of dry vermouth) are very potent. Bourbon, mellow whiskey distilled mostly in Kentucky, is made of corn, malt and rye; drink it straight, on the rocks or with soda. Many bars have a late-afternoon "happy hour" when they'll give you two drinks for the price of one or serve free snacks.

GASTRONOMICAL GAZETTEER

A steak may be a steak any way you slice it, but visitors to the city are sometimes confused by the local terminology.

The tender "New York cut", also called "sheet" or "strip steak", comes (appropriately) from the tenderloin. "London broil" did not cross the Atlantic with the pilgrims; it's a native American piece of flank or round cut against the grain. As for "Swiss steak", no yodelling, please. It's not even steak, but braised beef with onion and tomato sauce. And finally, don't expect anything chummy from "club steaks": they come from the rib, not select institutions.

Prices

Most restaurants charge more for dinner than for a comparable lunch. You can order just a salad if you like, but sometimes there is a minimum charge. Ask about the "special" (dish of the day). In many places you pay the cashier on your way out, after leaving the tip on the table.

BLUEPRINT FOR A PERFECT TRIP

CONTENTS

100 Accommodation
101 Airports
103 Baby-Sitters
103 Bicycle Rental (Hire)
103 Boat Excursions
103 Car Rental (Hire)
104 Climate
104 Clothing
104 Complaints
105 Consulates
105 Crime and Theft
105 Customs and Entry Formalities
106 Driving
108 Drugs
108 Electric Current
108 Emergencies
108 Getting to New York
109 Guides and Tours
109 Hairdresses and Barbers
109 Health and Medical Care
110 Language
110 Laundry and Dry-Cleaning
110 Liquor Regulations
111 Local Transport
112 Lost Property
112 Mail
113 Maps
113 Meeting People
113 Money Matters
114 Newspapers and Magazines
114 Photography
115 Planning Your Budget
116 Post Offices
116 Public Holidays, Parades and Festivals
117 Radio and TV
117 Religious Services
118 Smoking
118 Telegrams, Telex, Fax
118 Telephone
119 Theatre and Concert Tickets
119 Time Differences
120 Tipping
120 Toilets
120 Tourist Information Offices
121 Trains
121 Water
121 Weights and Measures

AN A–Z SUMMARY OF PRACTICAL INFORMATION

Certain items of information in this section will already be familiar to U.S. residents, but have been included to be of help to visitors from overseas.

ACCOMMODATION. The New York Convention & Visitors Bureau (see Tourist Information Offices) can give you an up-to-date list of hotels. You should book a room in advance if possible; the city can be very crowded during convention and holiday periods. Have your reservation confirmed before leaving for New York and bring it along with you. Rates do not include a tax of 19¼% (14¼% if the room rate is less than $100), plus a $2 per day occupancy tax. Unless you are on a prepaid tour, no meals will be included in the price of the room. At many hotels children can sleep in their parents' room at no extra charge.

Youth hostels. In addition to the youth hostel (see below), open to travellers of all ages, there are a number of residences run by the YMCA and the YWCA, commonly known as Ys. Hotel taxes are not charged for stays at the AYH or Ys. You don't have to belong to any special organization to stay in the Ys, but it's better to reserve a room by writing to the Resident Director. Two of the best Ys, open to both men and women, are:

Vanderbilt YMCA, 224 East 47th Street, New York, NY 10017 (tel. 755-2410)

West Side YMCA, 5 West 63rd Street, New York, NY 10023 (tel. 787-4400)

The New York International AYH-Hostel, 891 Amsterdam Avenue, New York, NY 10025 (tel. 932-2300)

Camping. Although there are no camp sites in New York City itself, you'll find a few on Long Island (such as Hither Hills at Montauk) and in the Hudson River Valley. Most open in May and close in September or

October. Remember to make advance reservations if it's for July or August. A booklet covering camping in New York State can be obtained from the New York Department of Commerce, Division of Tourism:

One Commerce Plaza, Albany, NY 12245

Within New York State, call 1-800-342-3810 (no charge); if phoning from another state, dial 1-518-474-4116 (toll call).

AIRPORTS. New York is served by three major airports—John F. Kennedy International Airport (JFK), LaGuardia Airport (LGA) and Newark International Airport (EWR). The majority of international flights land at Kennedy, where air traffic can be very heavy during peak flying times.

Arriving from abroad, you must first present your passport and immigration card to an immigration official. He or she will attach a temporary residence visa to your passport which must be given back when you leave the country. After you've collected your luggage, you take it through the red or green customs channel, depending on whether you have anything to declare, and hand the customs form over to the checker at the customs area exit.

Several private companies offer a convenient mini-bus service between the airports and midtown Manhattan hotels and offices. This shared door-to-door transport is more expensive than the scheduled services—ask at the airport terminal's Ground Transportation desk. Also available are (expensive) chauffeur-driven limousines. For information on taxis, see Local Transport.

Inter-airport bus connections exist between Kennedy and both LaGuardia and Newark.

Departing passengers should keep in mind that during rush hours, buses and taxis could take twice the normal time. If you go by bus, tell the driver which airline you're flying with so that he can let you off at the right terminal.

For detailed recorded information on transport to and from the three airports, call the Port Authority's toll-free number: 1-800-AIR-RIDE.

Kennedy Airport. Carey Transportation runs express coaches from all airport terminals to midtown Manhattan. Buses leave every 30 minutes for the Carey ticket office at 125 Park Avenue between East 41st and 42nd streets (opposite Grand Central Terminal) and continue to the Air TransCenter at Port Authority Bus Terminal (Eighth Avenue at West

42nd Street). A separate shuttle service operates from the Grand Central stop to major midtown hotels. The 15-mile trip from JFK takes from 60 to 75 minutes (longer at peak times).

A regular 20-minute helicopter service (New York Helicopter) links JFK (TWA International Terminal) to the heliport on East River at East 34th Street. Some airlines offer free or reduced rates—check with your carrier for details.

The least expensive means of transport (for the price of a token) is the subway. Catch the shuttle bus from any of JFK's terminals to the Howard Beach subway station, where the A train will take you to stops downtown, midtown and on the Upper West Side, including the Port Authority Bus Terminal.

LaGuardia Airport is also served by Carey coaches. They leave every 20 minutes for the same midtown addresses as the JFK buses. The 6-mile ride takes 45 minutes (longer at peak times).

Quick Trip LaGuardia Express buses connect the airport to the 21st Street–Queensbridge subway station, from where you can take the Q or B train to midtown.

A Pan Am Water Shuttle operates from LaGuardia's Marine Air Terminal down the East River to East 34th Street and Pier 11, just south of Wall Street. Ring 1-800-54-FERRY (toll-free) for schedule.

Newark Airport. New Jersey Transit buses leave every 15 to 30 minutes from all airport terminals for the Port Authority Bus Terminal (Manhattan). The 16-mile trip takes 30 to 45 minutes (longer in peak-hour traffic through the Lincoln Tunnel). Alternatively, take an Airlink Bus to Newark Penn Station (15 to 30 minutes' travel) and catch a New Jersey Transit or Amtrak train to New York Penn Station (Madison Square Garden) or the PATH (Port Authority Trans-Hudson) train to Sixth Avenue at West 33rd Street or to the World Trade Center in downtown Manhattan.

Olympia Trail Airport Express also runs scheduled airport express buses. These leave the terminals every 20 to 30 minutes for midtown Manhattan at West 34th Street (near Penn Station) and Park Avenue at East 41st Street (near Grand Central Terminal), as well as for 1 World Trade Center (near the West Street entrance). The midtown trip takes from 35 to 65 minutes, the downtown one 20 to 45 minutes.

Duty-free shops offer a wide range of articles. Your purchase will be delivered directly to the departure gate where you'll pick it up when boarding. Most shops refuse to take any orders less than half an hour before the take-off of your flight.

BABY-SITTERS. You should be able to obtain the names of baby-sitting agencies from the hotel receptionist, or consult the Yellow Pages of the telephone directory. The Baby Sitters' Guild can usually send someone over on short notice. Call morning or afternoon for an evening booking. There is a minimum number of hours, and you pay the sitter's car fare.

The Baby Sitters' Guild, 60 East 42nd Street; tel. 682-0227

BICYCLE RENTAL (HIRE). A list of rental agencies can be found in the Yellow Pages of the telephone directory under "Bicycles–Dealers, Repairers & Rental".

BOAT EXCURSIONS. Splendid views of the city are in store when you take one of a variety of boat trips around Manhattan.

From March to December the Circle Line leaves from Pier 83 at the foot of West 43rd Street for a 3-hour cruise around Manhattan, while the Seaport Line Harbor Cruises operate a narrated, 90-minute excursion aboard a replica paddleboat. Board at South Street Seaport. Or see Manhattan in 75 minutes from a catamaran, which leaves from Pier 11, near the bottom of Wall Street. Year-round you can take the ferry from Battery Park to the Statue of Liberty and Ellis Island. The Staten Island Ferry also leaves from Battery Park and offers an impressive view of Manhattan and the Statue of Liberty.

CAR RENTAL (HIRE). Cars can be hired at the airports or in New York City from one of many rental agencies (listed in the Yellow Pages under "Automobile Renting & Leasing"). Prices are competitive, and you can save a substantial amount of money if you shop around. If you want to be sure of obtaining a particular model at the airport, however, make arrangements through an international agency before leaving home. Most rental firms propose special weekend and unlimited-mileage rates; some offer rent-it-here, leave-it-there deals. It's a good idea to reserve a week in advance for weekend rentals from mid-May to mid-September.

Agencies prefer credit-card transactions. The minimum age for renting a car is normally 21. Many agencies require an International Driving Permit if the renter's national licence is in a language other than English. Anyway, an IDP (or your driving licence accompanied by a translation) is highly recommended in case of an encounter with a local policeman.

If you'd like to cross the country cheaply, look into an auto-drive-away deal. If you have references in America and you meet certain conditions, you may be engaged to drive someone else's car to a specified destination. A refundable security deposit is required, then the car is turned over to you with a tank of petrol. The driver pays all other expenses. For further information, contact Autodrive-away Co.:

264 West 35th Street, New York, NY 10001 (tel. 967-2344)

CLIMATE

Between October and March the days are usually clear. In summer you should expect periods of heat and humidity alleviated in part by air conditioning in shops, hotels and restaurants. The best seasons to visit New York are spring (April to May) and autumn (September to October).

Monthly average maximum and minimum daytime temperatures:

	J	F	M	A	M	J	J	A	S	O	N	D
max. °F	39	40	48	61	71	81	85	83	77	67	54	41
min. °F	26	27	34	44	53	63	68	66	60	51	41	30

CLOTHING. In New York you have to cope with extremes of temperature, not just between winter and summer, but even between outdoors and indoors. You'll find that most stores overheat in winter and overcool in summer.

In winter a heavy coat is a necessity. Under it wear several layers of lighter clothes, which can be shed according to the temperature indoors. Don't forget your winter boots, warm hat and gloves. Only Canadians could call New York winters mild.

In summer wear your lightest clothes, in natural fibres if possible. The air is so humid and sticky that you'll need several changes of clothing. Carry a sweater to ward off the chill you'll feel indoors in the frigid New York air conditioning. Bring along a raincoat, too, for you may well be caught in a downpour. Rubber overshoes are very practical and are sold in department stores and shoe shops.

COMPLAINTS. If you feel you have reason to complain about retail stores or business practices, you should contact New York City Department of Consumer Affairs:

80 Lafayette Street, New York, NY 10013 (tel. 577-0111)

For complaints about taxi drivers or taxi fares, see LOCAL TRANSPORT.

CONSULATES

Australia	630 Fifth Avenue; tel. 245-4000
Canada	1251 Avenue of the Americas; tel. 768-2400
Eire	515 Madison Avenue; tel. 319-2555
New Zealand	Washington, D.C.; tel. 1-202-328-4800
South Africa	326 East 48th Street; tel. 371-7997
United Kingdom	845 Third Avenue; tel. 745-0202

CRIME and THEFT. It's true that New York City's crime rate is high, that theft is common, and tourists are always easy targets for robbery. By taking a few simple precautions, you can reduce the risk:

- always lock your hotel room door
- deposit valuables in the hotel safe
- never carry large amounts of cash on you, and always wear a minimum of jewellery (watches, chains and even shoulder bags can easily be torn off)
- carry as much money as possible in the form of traveller's cheques, and keep a record of these (and your passport) separate from the cheques themselves
- avoid side streets or obviously seedy areas
- never leave valuables (bags, etc.) unattended or behind your back even for a few seconds

And if you *are,* in fact, robbed, don't play the hero; hand over what you have. Then report it to the police immediately (tel. 374-5000 or 911 for emergencies): your insurance company will need to see a copy of the police report (as will your consulate if your passport is stolen). As for stolen or lost traveller's cheques, report the matter at once to the bank that issued them so that payment can be stopped immediately.

CUSTOMS and ENTRY FORMALITIES. Also see Airports. To enter the United States, most foreign visitors need a valid passport and a visitor's visa, which can be obtained at any U.S. embassy or consulate. In general, British visitors with a valid ten-year passport and a return ticket purchased from one of the major airlines do not need a U.S. visa for stays of less than 90 days. Canadians only need to present proof of nationality. Everyone must fill out customs declaration forms before arrival (usually distributed by your airline near the end of the flight).

The following chart shows certain duty-free items you may take into the U.S. (if you are over 21) and, when returning home, into your own country:

Into:	Cigarettes		Cigars		Tobacco	Spirits		Wine
U.S.A.	200	or	50	or	1,350 g.	1 l.	or	1 l.
Australia	200	or	250	or	250 g.	1 l.	or	1 l.
Canada	200	and	50	and	900 g.	1.1 l.	or	1.1 l.
Eire	200	or	50	or	250 g.	1 l.	and	2 l.
N. Zealand	200	or	50	or	250 g.	1.1 l.	and	4.5 l.
S. Africa	400	and	50	and	250 g.	1 l.	and	2 l.
U.K.	200	or	50	or	250 g.	1 l.	and	2 l.

A non-resident may claim, free of duty and taxes, articles up to $100 in value for use as gifts for other persons. The exemption is valid only if the gifts accompany you, if you stay 72 hours or more and have not claimed this exemption within the preceding 6 months. Up to 100 cigars may be included within this gift exemption.

Arriving and departing passengers must report any money or cheques, etc., exceeding a total of $10,000.

DRIVING

Driving conditions. Although New York City is best avoided by car, you may wish to explore Long Island, Connecticut or other surrounding areas. If you *must* drive a car in New York City, remember certain rules: the speed limit is 30 m.p.h. unless otherwise indicated; you may not use your horn in town; the use of seat belts is mandatory in the state of New York; and, of course, visitors from the U.K. must remember to drive on the right. Be sure you are fully insured; if you are responsible for an accident, fines can be high.

Parking. The city has a considerable number of car parks (listed in the Yellow Pages under "Parking Stations & Garages"). It's a good idea to use them, since it's next to impossible to find a place to park on the street. If you do happen to find one, obey posted parking regulations. Never park next to a fire hydrant and don't leave your car on the street over the time limit, or it may be towed away—a costly proposition!

Highways, bridges and tunnels. There are several terms used for different types of highways, and some of these (except for expressways) collect tolls. Toll highways may be called "thruways", "parkways" (usually lined with shrubs, flowers or trees) or "turnpikes". You should keep a stock of change for convenience when travelling; most toll areas have baskets for drivers with correct change; you simply drop in the right amount so there's no waiting. The speed limit on most highways is 55 m.p.h. Limits are strictly enforced.

In New York there are 65 bridges; tolls of varying amounts must be paid on many of them. Tolls are also payable for the tunnels serving Manhattan.

Petrol. Service stations are few and far between in the city. They are often open in the evening and on Sundays.

Breakdowns and insurance. The Automobile Club of New York (ACNY), a branch of the American Automobile Association (AAA), will help members, as well as foreign visitors affiliated with other recognized automobile associations. In case of breakdown or for other problems along the way, call their Emergency Road Service on 757-3356; or wait until a state police patrol car comes along.

ACNY: 1881 Broadway; tel. 586-1166

AAA: 28 East 78th Street; tel. 586-1166

The AAA also offers information on travelling in the U.S., as well as short-term insurance for visitors (1 to 12 months).

AAA World Wide Travel, AAA Drive, Heathrow, FL 32746-5063 (tel. 1-407-444-7000)

Road signs. You will encounter some international road signs, but you may see the following written signs as well:

American	British
Detour	Diversion
Divided highway	Dual carriageway
No passing	No overtaking
No parking along highway	Clearway
Railroad crossing	Level crossing
Roadway	Carriageway
Traffic circle	Roundabout
Yield	Give way

DRUGS. The possession of any drugs—hard or soft—is usually considered a jailable offence. For a foreigner, it may mean expulsion from the U.S., and expulsion for life, without mentioning the possibility of horrendous fines.

ELECTRIC CURRENT. 110 volt 60-cycle A.C. is standard throughout the U.S. Plugs are the flat, two-pronged variety. Foreign visitors without dual-voltage appliances will need a transformer and adaptor plug for their electric razors, hair dryers and travel irons.

EMERGENCIES

All-purpose emergency number	911
Dentist Emergency Service	679-3966
Doctors On Call	1-718-238-2100

The telephone operator can also connect you with emergency services, dial "0".

GETTING TO NEW YORK

From the United States and Canada

By Air: There is a daily service between New York City and at least one city in every state of the union as well as from Toronto and Montreal. Major U.S. cities are linked with New York by hourly non-stop flights during the day. Fares change constantly, so it would be wise to consult an airline or travel agency for the latest information about discounts and special deals.

By Bus: The major metropolitan centres in North America have regular bus connections with New York City. The only requirement is that the destination be reached within 60 days after the ticket is purchased. You save approximately 10% on round-trip tickets. Greyhound Trailways Bus Lines offer flat-rate rover passes for specified periods of unlimited travel.

You can also take a scheduled escorted tour to New York City from the South or Midwest. Daily stops allow for sightseeing and meals. Transportation, hotel rooms, baggage handling, sightseeing and admission charges are usually included in the price.

By Rail: Amtrak trains, with dining-car service and slumber-coach, roomette or bedroom accommodation, link New York City with the West Coast.

Amtrak features the U.S.A. Railpass for unlimited travel at a flat rate for given periods of time. They also offer package tours to New York which include travel and hotel accommodation.

The Montrealer runs from Montreal to New York, with excellent connections from other parts of Canada.

From the United Kingdom and Eire

By Air: Because of the complexity of the many new fares, you need the advice of an informed travel agent well before your holiday. Apart from the standard first-class and economy fares, the main types of fares available are the Super APEX, Special Economy and Standby.

From Australia and New Zealand

From Australia: There's a twice-weekly air service from Sydney to New York via Los Angeles. Package deals, excursion fares and APEX fares are available.

From New Zealand: Scheduled flights leave daily for New York from Auckland via Los Angeles. Excursion fares allow intermediate stops. EPIC fares do not permit stopovers.

GUIDES and TOURS. Several agencies offer organized tours and special excursions (helicopter, nightclub rounds, historical tours, etc.). Individual sightseeing guides are also available. For details, contact the New York Convention & Visitors Bureau:

2 Columbus Circle, New York, NY 10019 (tel. 397-8222)

HAIRDRESSERS and BARBERS. There are plenty of barbers, and women's hairdressers usually accept male customers as well. During the week you can be fitted in fairly promptly in most establishments, but you should book ahead for a Saturday appointment.

HEALTH and MEDICAL CARE. Also see EMERGENCIES. Arrangements for temporary health and accident insurance should be made beforehand through your travel agency or an insurance company, or ask at your local Social Security office for precise information on coverage during your trip to the States. Tourists can purchase additional short-term insurance for journeys within the U.S. at the insurance counters and from the vending machines to be found everywhere in air, bus and rail terminals.

Except in an emergency, foreign visitors should call their consulate for a list of doctors in New York City. In any emergency, medical or otherwise, local telephone operators are an excellent source of advice.

Drugstores. A prescription is required for many medicines. There are numerous drugstores, but only one in the central Manhattan area is open day and night, 7 days a week:

Kaufman's Pharmacy, Lexington Avenue at East 50th Street; tel. 755-2266

LANGUAGE. Certain words have different meanings for the Americans and the British. Here are a few which could be a source of confusion:

U.S.	British	U.S.	British
admission	entry fee	**liquor store**	off-licence
bathroom	toilet (private)	**pavement**	road surface
bill	note (money)	**rest room**	toilet (public)
billfold	wallet	**round-trip (ticket)**	return
check	bill (restaurant)	**second floor**	first floor
collect call	reverse charges	**sidewalk**	pavement
elevator	lift	**stand in line**	queue up
first floor	ground floor	**subway**	underground
gasoline	petrol	**trailer**	caravan
liquor	spirits	**underpass**	subway

LAUNDRY and DRY-CLEANING. Your hotel may have efficient same-day service and some even provide drying lines in the bathroom.

You can also find self-service laundries where coin-operated washing machines and dryers are available. Look under "Laundries–Self-Service" in the Manhattan Yellow Pages or ask your hotel receptionist.

Dry-cleaners usually provide one-day service. They are also listed in the telephone directory's Yellow Pages under "Cleaners & Dyers". Self-service dry-cleaners ("Cleaners–Self-Service"), where you pay according to weight, are well-run; each load takes about an hour.

LIQUOR REGULATIONS. Most alcoholic beverages are sold exclusively in licensed liquor stores. In Manhattan beer can be bought in licensed supermarkets and grocery stores. Small restaurants that don't have the expensive permit to serve liquor will usually let you bring your own bottle of wine.

Most liquor stores are open until 9 or 10 p.m., sometimes even until midnight. They are not open on Sunday (beer is sold on Sunday after midday). Another carry-over from Prohibition is the law that bottles (or beer cans) must be concealed when drinking in public. The minimum age for drinking any alcoholic beverage is 21.

LOCAL TRANSPORT

Bus and subway maps are available free at the token booths at major subway stations, the information booths at Grand Central Terminal and Port Authority Bus Terminal, as well as at the New York Convention & Visitors Bureau. For assistance on bus and subway routes you can also call the New York City Transport Authority on 1-718-330-1234.

Children under 44 inches tall travel free.

Buses. In Manhattan all public buses are numbered and bear the prefix M. They either follow the avenues or run crosstown along the major streets.

Bus stops, not easily spotted, are indicated by a signpost showing a red-and-white "No standing" sign, a blue-and-white bus logo and the bus number. Some stops have a glass-enclosed shelter with Guide-A-Ride route maps and schedules. Avenue buses usually stop at every second or third block, while crosstown buses generally stop at the corner of each avenue. Drivers have to be hailed.

Enter by the front door and deposit a token (available at subway stations only) or the exact change (no banknotes) in the box next to the driver. A free transfer ticket is available for bus routes that intersect or continue the route (ask for a "Transfer" when boarding).

Subway. This is the fastest means of transport in New York. It operates 24 hours a day, but not all trains run at all times. You can purchase tokens from the booth located in each station. However, some booths close at night, so buy a handful or "10-pack" of tokens at a time. Try to avoid the subway at rush hours (6–9.30 a.m. and 4–7 p.m.).

In Manhattan the vast majority of lines go north–south. For crosstown travel you may have to change trains. Once you have entered the subway network by depositing a token at the entrance turnstile, you may travel to any destination, changing trains as required. If you're uncertain about which line to take, consult the back of the subway map which shows the layout of each individual route. You can also enquire at the token booth. Unless you are sure that the train stops at your destination, you are better off catching a "local" rather than an "express". Local trains are slow, but they are also generally less crowded.

Scheduled services are subject to change. Be sure to check any notices for diversions and up-to-date information.

During the day the subway is generally safe. However, never wait on the edge of the platform and, if the platform is empty, wait as close as possible to the token booth. At night it's safer to take a taxi.

Taxis. Fares are clearly marked in black on the door. A small surcharge is made at night (8 p.m.–6 a.m.) and on Sundays, though it doesn't show up on the meter. The driver is entitled to charge extra for baggage, but most don't bother. If your route comprises a toll tunnel or bridge, you must pay the toll.

Should you have a complaint to make about a driver, note his name and number and contact the NYC Taxi and Limousine Commission (tel. 221-8294).

Avoid taxis without a medallion no matter what discount they may offer. Legally, only the yellow cars with numbers on the roof are allowed to pick up passengers in the streets.

If you're nervous about getting to the airport on time, you can book a cab through one of the private companies listed in the Yellow Pages under "Taxicab Service".

Taxi drivers have no obligation to change banknotes of denominations higher than $5 (it's more than wise to have with you at all times some $1 banknotes—they constantly come in handy). You should give the driver a tip of at least 15%, more for special service.

LOST PROPERTY. Each transport system maintains its own lost-property office. It's reassuring to know that even in New York, dozens of items are turned in daily, sometimes valuable ones.

New York City Transit Authority (NYCTA) Lost Property Office (subway network and bus system): tel. 1-718-625-6200

NYC Taxi & Limousine Commission Lost Property: tel. 1-718-840-4734

MAIL. If you don't know where you'll be staying in New York, you can have mail sent to you c/o General Delivery (poste restante) to the General Post Office:

421 Eighth Avenue, New York, NY 10001

American Express will also accept mail for foreign visitors (without charge if you hold their credit card or traveller's cheques); envelopes should be marked "Client's Mail".

The mail should be collected within 90 days. Take your passport along for identification.

MAPS. At the New York Convention & Visitors Bureau tourists can get a free map of Manhattan. Public transport route maps are available at the toll booth in subway stations. Falk, who provided the maps for this book, also publishes a complete series of detailed New York area maps.

MEETING PEOPLE. Central Park on Sunday is the place to do it—or one of the countless "mixer" bars and other night spots. Don't be surprised if strangers in elevators start up a conversation, as Americans tend to be outgoing.

Like city dwellers everywhere, New Yorkers are often tense and in a hurry. In a restaurant or the post office, your "Thank you" may only meet with a grunt in reply. It's quite usual and means "Not at all". Even Americans from outside the city are amazed at the self-absorption of New Yorkers. The only answer to your questions in the street may be a shrug. However, at gatherings (such as parties) New Yorkers show themselves to be friendly and interested in meeting people.

MONEY MATTERS

Currency. The dollar is divided into 100 cents.

Coins: 1¢ (penny), 5¢ (nickel), 10¢ (dime), 25¢ (quarter), 50¢ (half-dollar; rare) and $1 (rare).

Banknotes: $1, $5, $10, $20, $50 and $100. All denominations are the same size and same black and green colour, so be sure to double-check your cash before you spend it.

For currency restrictions, see CUSTOMS and ENTRY FORMALITIES.

Banks and currency exchange. Most banks are open weekdays from 9 a.m. to 3 p.m. (often till 6 p.m. on Thursdays).

If you arrive on the weekend, be sure to change some money before leaving the airport, where currency exchange offices remain open. You may be able to change money at your hotel, though you probably won't get the bank rate. Note that banks usually prefer to change only small sums of foreign money.

Visitors from abroad should bear in mind that foreign money cannot be changed in most banks; you have to go to certain ones, like Citibank. Therefore, it's best to carry dollars with you, in cash or traveller's cheques. There are, however, a number of companies specializing in foreign currency exchange; look them up in the Yellow Pages under the heading "Foreign Money Brokers and Dealers".

Make sure you always have a supply of $1 banknotes (for taxis, toll bridges, tipping, etc.)—they are invariably useful.

Credit cards. The major cards are accepted as cash almost everywhere. When paying for goods or services, including hotel and restaurant bills, you will be asked: "Cash or charge?", meaning you have the choice of paying either in cash or in "plastic money".

Traveller's cheques. Visitors from abroad will find traveller's cheques drawn on American banks far easier to deal with. Only cash small amounts at a time, and keep the balance of your cheques in the hotel safe if possible. At the very least, be sure to keep your receipt and a list of the serial numbers of the cheques in a separate place to facilitate a refund in case of loss or theft.

Sales tax. Expect to have state and city taxes, a total of 8¼%, added to the marked-up price of all goods purchased in New York City, including meals.

NEWSPAPERS and MAGAZINES. The city's major newspapers are the *Daily News, The New York Times* and the *New York Post.* The Sunday *New York Times* includes a particularly comprehensive arts and leisure section, useful for visitors. The weekly publications—*The New Yorker, New York* and *The Village Voice*—are helpful for finding out what's going on in theatres, nightclubs, museums, art galleries, concert halls and in the world of sport.

For the best selection of foreign newspapers and magazines, go to Hotalings at 142 West 42nd Street or the newsstands in the lobbies of larger hotels.

PHOTOGRAPHY. All popular brands of film and photographic equipment are available. Try to buy in discount stores where prices are much lower.

Airport X-ray machines do not normally affect ordinary film, but ask for hand inspection of high-speed film. Protect any film in a lightweight insulating bag.

The staff at Nikon House will gladly advise you about equipment. While you're there you may want to have a look at the current exhibition of photography, at 620 Fifth Avenue (tel. 586-3907).

PLANNING YOUR BUDGET

To give you an idea of what to expect, here's a list of average prices in U.S. dollars. They can only be *approximate,* however, as inflation creeps up relentlessly.

Airport transfer. Taxi (excluding tolls and tip) from JFK to Manhattan about $30, from LaGuardia $23, from Newark International Airport $35. Bus from JFK to Grand Central Terminal or Port Authority Bus Terminal (Air TransCenter) $9.50, from LaGuardia $7.50, from Newark International to Port Authority or World Trade Center $7, to the centre of Newark $4.

Baby-sitters. $10–12.50 per hour (4 hours min.) for 1 child, plus transport ($4.50 up to midnight, $7 after midnight).

Bicycle rental (hire). $4–7 per hour (depending on whether 3- or 10-speed), $18–27 for full day, deposit $20.

Buses. $1.15 a trip, including transfer on certain lines (but you must ask for it when you pay). Exact change or token is required.

Car rental (hire). It's impossible to give a range of average rental charges as prices vary enormously, depending on the season and the firm. The cheaper weekly rates advertised by many companies apply only when a car is reserved a week in advance.

Cigarettes (packet of 20). $1.85 and up, plus tax.

Entertainment. Cinema $6–7. Theatre $25–60 on Broadway, $10–40 Off-Broadway. Ballet, concerts $5–45. Nightclub $5–50.

Guided tours. City bus tour $14–33. Circle Line boat trip around Manhattan $15, children under 12 $7.50. Walking tour of New York $1–15 per person. Atlantic City day trip $20–25.

Hairdressers. Woman's haircut and blow-dry $18 and up, shampoo and set or blow-dry $12 and up. Man's haircut and blow-dry at barber shops $10 and up, at hairdressers $20 and up.

Hotels (double occupancy per night), tax not included. Budget category up to $100, moderate $100–200, luxury $200–700.

Restaurants (tax not included). Breakfast $5 and up, lunch in coffee shop $7 and up, in restaurant $12 and up, dinner $18 and up, glass of wine $2.50 and up, bottle of wine $15 and up, glass of beer $2.50 and up, whisky $3.50 and up, soft drink $1.50 and up, coffee $1 and up.

Subway. Token $1.15.

Taxis. Meter starts at $1.50; there's a charge of 25 cents per 1/5 mile of travel; 25 cents per 75 seconds waiting time and a night surcharge of 50 cents (8 p.m.–6 a.m.).

Youth hostels (YMCA, per night). Double room $42–52, single room $28–44; The New York International AYH-Hostel: about $20 per person.

POST OFFICES. The U.S. Post Office only deals with mail. Branches are generally open weekdays from 8 a.m. to 5 p.m. and on Saturday from 9 a.m. to 1 p.m. The New York's General Post Office (see p. 112) stays open 24 hours.

You can buy stamps at the reception desk in your hotel or from stamp machines (often found in public buildings or stores where stationery is sold). Stamps sold by machine may cost more than at the post office. You'll find the standard blue mailboxes on almost every street.

PUBLIC HOLIDAYS, PARADES and FESTIVALS. In New York banks and most stores are closed on the following holidays:

Holiday	Date
New Year's Day	January 1
Martin Luther King Day*	Third Monday in January
President's Day*	Third Monday in February
Memorial Day	Last Monday in May
Independence Day	July 4
Labor Day	First Monday in September
Columbus Day*	Second Monday in October
Veterans' Day*	November 11
Thanksgiving Day	Fourth Thursday in November
Christmas Day	December 25

* Partially or optionally observed.

Parades. St. Patrick's Day (patron saint of Ireland) on March 17. Fifth Avenue is the scene of the action with some great Irish hospitality.

The **Easter Parade** meanders up Fifth Avenue from St. Patrick's Cathedral. A good chance to see the best and worst in American fashion.

The **Columbus Day** parade, on the second Monday in October, is primarily an Italian affair, but the rest of New York turns out to watch.

The **Thanksgiving** parade, on the fourth Thursday of November, is held on Broadway. This is *the* parade for kids.

Festivals. The **Chinese New Year** is a movable feast occurring in January or February. Go to Chinatown if you're not frightened by the racket—the pavements are minefields of firecrackers, noisy but harmless.

The **Feast of St. Anthony of Padua** in early June (on Sullivan Street between Houston and Prince streets) and the **Feast of San Gennaro** in September (on Mulberry and Grand streets in Little Italy) both feature fun, games and Italian street food.

Also during the summer, **music festivals** are held throughout the city. Some of the major ones are the Metropolitan Opera's park concerts in June, the Jazz Festival at the end of June (in various halls), the Summerpier concerts at South Street Seaport (July–August), the New York Philharmonic's park concerts (July–August), the Washington Square Music Festival (classic) in Greenwich Village (July–August) and the Greenwich Village Jazz Festival (August–September).

And, most patriotically, New York celebrates Independence Day, July 4, with festivals and spectacular fireworks.

RADIO and TV. You'll almost certainly have a radio and television in your hotel room, with a vast choice of programmes.

It's difficult to choose among all the radio programmes. In New York there are about 60 AM-FM stations.

Television stations broadcast from 6 a.m. until around 3 or 4 the next morning. The national networks (channels 2, 4, 5 and 7) and some cable channels transmit programmes round-the-clock. Channel 13, the Public Broadcasting Service, has no commercials. The major news broadcasts can be watched at 6 a.m. and 7 p.m.

RELIGIOUS SERVICES. Every conceivable religion is represented in New York; not only the well-known faiths but a large number of offbeat sects also hold services.

Houses of worship are listed in the Manhattan Yellow Pages under "Churches". A list of the main churches is also posted in most hotel lobbies.

Here's a cross section for different beliefs:

Catholic: St. Patrick's Cathedral, Fifth Avenue between East 50th and 51st streets (opposite Rockefeller Center); tel. 753-2261

Episcopalian: Cathedral Church of St. John the Divine, Amsterdam Avenue at West 112th Street; tel. 316-7540

Jewish: Temple Emanu-El, East 65th Street at Fifth Avenue; tel. 744-1400

Methodist: Lexington United Methodist Church, 150 East 62nd Street; tel. 838-6915

Moslem: Islamic Center of New York, East 96th Street between Second and Third avenues; tel. 362-6800

Presbyterian: Central Presbyterian Church, 593 Park Avenue; tel. 838-0808

Zen Studies Society: 223 East 67th Street; tel. 861-3333

SMOKING. Cigarettes vary in price depending on where you buy them. A packet from a vending machine always costs much more than one obtained in a supermarket or at a newsstand. Cigarettes are cheaper when bought by the carton.

The choice of pipe tobacco, both home-grown and imported, is vast, though you won't find any from Cuba as it's not available in the U.S.

Smoking is prohibited in many public places, including subway trains and stations. Restaurants in New York have smoking and no-smoking sections; in some, smoking is prohibited.

TELEGRAMS, TELEX, FAX. American telegraph companies are privately run. The main companies, such as RCA and Western Union (Western Union International for overseas), are listed in the Yellow Pages directory under "Telegraph Companies". Cablegrams (international telegrams) and telexes may be telephoned, expensively, from your hotel room. If you have an internationally accepted credit card, pick up any public phone and give them your message, and it will be billed to your card. Or go to one of their offices and pay them cash or by credit card. For fax messages, look up in the Yellow Pages under "Facsimile Transmission Service" or go to a stationery store displaying a "Fax Service" sign.

TELEPHONE. Directions for use are on the instrument. Telephone rates are listed and explained in the front of the White Pages of the telephone directory. Also included is information on person-to-person (personal) calls, collect (reverse-charge) calls, conference, station-to-station and credit-card calls. All numbers with an 800 prefix are toll-free (no charge). There are reductions for phoning at night, on weekends and on holidays.

New York has two area codes: 212 for Manhattan and the Bronx, 718 for Queens, Brooklyn and Staten Island. So if you are in Manhattan and want to telephone a subscriber in Brooklyn, you have to dial 1-718 + subscriber's number to get through (but still at the same charge as for a local call).

Long-distance call charges are calculated per minute; direct-dialling is the easiest and fastest method even from a phone booth. After 3 minutes the operator will interrupt to tell you to add more money. If you need assistance, dial "0" and ask for an overseas operator.

Some useful numbers:

Parks (special events, usually free)	360-1333	Time	967-1616
		Weather	976-1212

THEATRE and CONCERT TICKETS. Seats for new or nearly new Broadway shows can be very difficult to obtain, particularly for the musicals. Ask at your hotel desk: the receptionist may be able to get you tickets for a small commission. There are countless ticket agencies in the Broadway/Times Square neighbourhood, or you can try at the theatre box office itself. Agencies are listed in the Yellow Pages under "Ticket Sales–Entertainment and Sports". If you have a major credit card, you can book tickets by phone and pick them up at the theatre on presentation of the card.

TKTS (Times Square Theatre Center), at Broadway and West 47th Street, is a non-profit-making organization that sells tickets on the day of the performance at slightly over half price. They are open from 10 a.m. for matinées (noon on Sunday) and from 3 till 8 p.m. for evening performances. Get there early, as the queue may be quite long; but the savings are well worth the wait. The TKTS booth in 2 World Trade Center handles tickets for evening shows only (weekdays 11 a.m.–5.30 p.m., Sat. 11 a.m.–1 p.m.). Queues here are shorter.

The Bryant Park Music and Dance Booth (West 42nd Street at Sixth Avenue) sells half-price tickets for concerts and dance performances the same day. Payment must be made in cash or traveller's cheques. The booth opens daily from about noon to 7 p.m.

TIME DIFFERENCES. The continental United States has a total of four time zones; New York City is on Eastern Standard Time. In summer (between April and October) Daylight Saving Time is adopted and clocks move ahead an hour.

The following chart shows the time in various cities in winter when it's noon in New York City:

Los Angeles	**New York**	London	Sydney
9 a.m.	**noon**	5 p.m.	4 a.m.
Sunday	**Sunday**	Sunday	Monday

Dates in the U.S. are written differently from those in Great Britain; for example: 1/6/99 means January 6, 1999.

TIPPING. Service is never included in a restaurant bill, but is sometimes added to it. The usual tip is 15% (an easy way to work it out is to double the 8¼% tax marked on your bill). Cinema or theatre ushers and filling-station attendants are not tipped. In general, porters are tipped $1 per bag, hotel maids $1 per day or $5 per week, guides 10–15%, lavatory attendants 50¢, taxi drivers and hairdressers 15%.

TOILETS. You can find toilets in restaurants, museums, railway stations and large stores. In some places you must deposit a dime, in others you should leave a tip for the attendant.

TOURIST INFORMATION OFFICES. New York Convention & Visitors Bureau is a non-profit-making organization subsidized by the city's hotels and merchants. The staff will give you city maps and leaflets about principal tourist attractions, a price list of major hotels and any further information you may require:

2 Columbus Circle, New York, NY 10019 (tel. 397-8222).
Hours: weekdays 9 a.m.–6 p.m.; Sat., Sun. 10 a.m.–6 p.m.

Travelers' Aid Society dispenses just about everything, even—for the traveller in distress who looks a serious enough proposition—pocket money. In New York City it's located at:

158 West 42nd Street; tel. 944-0013

The Automobile Club of New York (ACNY) offers helpful advice on motoring in the U.S. They also give information on how to get to your destination by car or public transport. Call 757-2000.

For information prior to arrival in the U.S., contact:

United States Travel Service, 22 Sackville Street, London W1;
tel. (071) 439 74 33

TRAINS. Amtrak (National Railroad Passenger Corporation) offers U.S.A. Railpasses (flat-rate unlimited rail travel for a given period of time). Various package deals are also available through Amtrak for link-ups with car rental agencies, bus companies and hotel groups—even so-called "railsail" packages, connecting with Caribbean cruises.

If you are going to one of the major cities along the Northeast Corridor (Boston, Philadelphia, Baltimore, Washington), you may prefer Amtrak's Metroliner Service, fast (New York–Washington 2h. 55 min., Boston 4h. 20 min.) luxury trains with reserved seating in club cars (meals and beverages served at the seat) or leg-rest coaches. In New York, seats may be booked by calling toll-free 1-800-523-8720 for the Metroliner Service, 582-6875 for all other Amtrak services. For reservations and information at other points nationwide, call toll-free 1-800-USA-RAIL (or 1-800-872-7245 in digits).

Pick up the ticket at the railway station counter. For trains with unreserved seating, a penalty is charged on tickets bought on the train when the station ticket office is open at the time of departure. Children under 2 travel free; from 2 to 11 included, half fare is charged.

In New York City there are three main stations: **Penn** (Pennsylvania) **Station**, underneath Madison Square Garden at West 34th Street and Eighth Avenue, is the most important for long-distance travel and also serves Long Island and New Jersey commuters. **Grand Central Station**, on East 42nd Street between Park and Lexington avenues, has suburban lines. **PATH stations**, for trains to New Jersey, are located below the World Trade Center, at Christopher Street and along Avenue of the Americas.

WATER. New York water is perfectly safe to drink. Mineral ("spring") water, both fizzy ("sparkling") and still ("natural"), can be bought in grocery stores.

WEIGHTS and MEASURES. The United States is one of the last countries in the world to change over to the metric system and is not yet involved in an official changeover programme.

Milk and fruit juice can be bought by the quart or half gallon, but wine and spirits now come in litre bottles. Food products usually have the weight marked in ounces and pounds as well as in grammes.

There are some slight differences between British and American measures, for instance:

1 U.S. gallon = 0.833 British Imp. gallon = 3.8 litres
1 U.S. quart = 0.833 British Imp. quart = 0.9 litres

Subways

Broadway-7 Avenue (West Side IRT)

1 Local Weekdays, 6:00–20:00, all stops, South Ferry to 137 St; skip-stop with 9, 137 to 242 St. All stops to 242 St, evenings, weekends, & nights
2 Express All times, uptown to 241 St, Bronx, downtown to Flatbush Av, Brooklyn
3 Express Daily, 6:00–24:00, uptown to 148 St, Manhattan, downtown to New Lots Av, Brooklyn. Nights, shuttle bus, 135–148 St
9 Local Weekdays only, 6:00–20:00; see 1

Lexington Avenue (East Side IRT)

4 Express All times, uptown to Woodlawn, Bronx, downtown to Atlantic, New Lots, or Utica Av, Brooklyn. Nights, 4 makes all local stops
5 Express Daily, 6:00–24:00, uptown to Dyre Av or 241 St, Bronx, downtown to Bowling Green, Manhattan, or Flatbush Av, Brooklyn
6 Local Daily, 6:00–24:00, uptown to Pelham Bay Park or East 177 St, Bronx, downtown to Brooklyn Bridge, Manhattan

Flushing-42 Street Crosstown (IRT)

7 Local All times, Main St, Queens, to Times Square, Manhattan; weekday express, 6:00– 20:00

42 Street Shuttle (IRT)

S All times, Grand Central to Times Square

8 Avenue (IND)

A Express Weekdays, 6:00–20:00, uptown to 207 St, Manhattan, downtown to Lefferts Blvd or Far Rockaway, Queens. Evenings, nights and weekends, all local stops
C Local Weekdays, 6:00–20:00, 145 St, Manhattan, or Bedford Park Blvd, Bronx, to Euclid Av, Brooklyn, or Rockaway Park, Queens. Evenings & weekends, 145 St to World Trade Center
E Local All times between Jamaica Center, Queens, and World Trade Center, Manhattan

6 Avenue (IND)

B Express Weekdays, 6:00–20:00, uptown to 168 St, Manhattan, downtown to Coney Island, Brooklyn. Evenings and weekends, between 21 St, Queens, and Coney Island, Brooklyn
D Express All times, uptown to 205 St, Bronx, downtown to Coney Island, Brooklyn
F Local Daily, 6:00–24:00, 179 St, Queens, to Kings Highway or Coney Island, Brooklyn. Nights, 50 St, Manhattan, to Coney Island
Q Local Weekdays, 6:00–21:00, 21 St, Queens, to Brighton Beach, Brooklyn; nights, 21 St, Queens, to Broadway-Lafayette St, Manhattan

Canarsie-14 Street Crosstown (BMT)

L All times, Canarsie, Bklyn–8 Av, Manhattan

Nassau Street (BMT)

J Local All times between Jamaica Center, Queens, and Broad St, Manhattan
M Local Weekdays, 6:00–20:00, Metropolitan Av, Queens, to Broad St, Manhattan
Z Local Rush hours, Jamaica to Broad St

Broadway (BMT)

N Local All times, Ditmars Blvd, Queens, to Coney Island, Bklyn
R Local Daily, 6:00–24:00, 71 Av or 179 St, Queens, to 95 St, Brooklyn

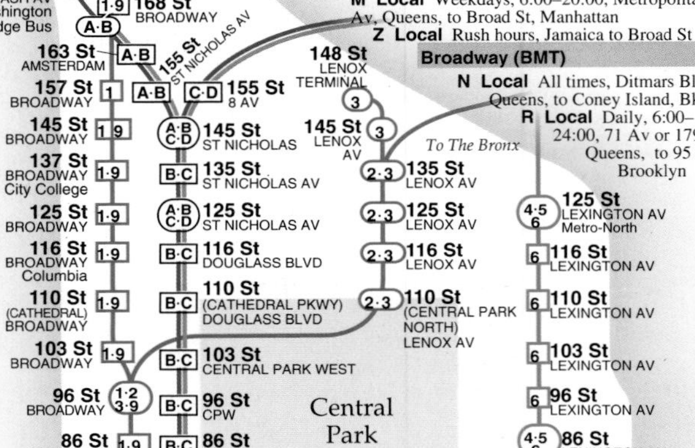

Central Park
Hudson River
East River
Roosevelt Island
To Queens
To Brooklyn
86 St BROADWAY 1·9
86 St CPW B·C
86 St LEX AV 4·5 6
79 St BROADWAY 1·9
81 St CPW Amer Museum Nat Hist B·C
77 St LEXINGTON AV 6
72 St BROADWAY 1·2 3·9
72 St CENTRAL PARK WEST B·C
68 St LEX AV-Hunter 6
66 St BROADWAY Lincoln Center 1·9
Lex Av 63 St B·Q
5 Av PLAZA N R
Lexington Av 60 St N R
59 St COLUMBUS CIRCLE A·B C·D 1·9
59 St LEXINGTON AV 4·5 6
7 Av 53 ST B D E
57 St 7 AV N R
57 St 6 AV B·Q
5 Av 53 ST E F
Lex-3 Avs 53 St E F
50 St 8 AV C·E
50 St BWAY 1·9
49 St 7 AV N R
47-50 Sts 6 AV-Rock Ctr B·D F·Q
51 St LEXINGTON AV 6
42 St 8 AV Port Auth Bus A·C E
42 St TIMES SQ N·R·1 2·3·7·9
S
7
5 Av 42 ST
42 St 6 AV B·D F·Q
42 St GRAND CENTRAL Metro-North Amtrak 4·5 6·7
34 St 8 AV PENN STA LIRR NJ Transit Amtrak A·C E
34 St 7 AV PENN 1·2 3·9
34 St HERALD SQ B·D·F N·Q·R PATH
33 St PARK AV 6
28 St 7 AV 1·9
28 St BWAY N R
28 St PARK AV SOUTH 6
23 St 8 AV C·E
23 St 7 AV 1·9
23 St 6 AV PATH F
23 St BWAY N R
23 St PARK AV S 6
14 St 8 AV A·C E
8 Av L
18 St 7 AV 1·9
6 Av 14 ST L
14 St 6 AV PATH F
14 St 7 AV 1·2 3·9
14 St-UNION SQ N·R L 4·5·6
3 Av-14 ST L
1 Av-14 ST L
8 St BWAY N R
Astor Place 8 ST-4 AV Cooper Union 6
West 4 St 6 AV-NYU A·B·C·D E·F·Q
Christopher St SHERIDAN SQ 7 AV SOUTH 1 9
Broadway-Lafayette HOUSTON B D F Q
Bleecker St LAFAYETTE ST 6 6
2 Av HOUSTON F
Houston St VARICK ST 1 9
Prince BWAY N R
Spring 6 AV C E
Spring LAFAYETTE 6
Bowery CHRYSTIE J M
Delancey St F
Essex St J M Z
Canal St VARICK ST 1 9
Canal 6 AV A·C E
Canal St BWAY-LAFAYETTE-CENTRE N R 6 J M·Z
Grand CHRYSTIE B D Q
East Broadway CANAL F
Franklin St VARICK ST 1 9
Chambers St WEST BROADWAY 1·2 3·9
Chambers St CHURCH A·C
City Hall BWAY N·R
Chambers St CENTRE ST J·M·Z
Brooklyn Bridge-City Hall CENTRE ST 4·5 6
World Trade Center VESEY-CHURCH STS PATH C·E
Park Place 2·3
Broadway-Nassau A·C
Cortlandt CHURCH N R
Fulton St BWAY-NASSAU- WILLIAM J·M·Z 2·3·4·5
Cortlandt St World Trade Ctr PATH 1 9
Wall BWAY 4 5
Wall St WILLIAM ST 2·3
Rector TRINITY PL N R
Rector St GREENWICH STREET 1 9
Broad St WALL ST J M Z
Bowling Green BROADWAY 4 5
Whitehall St WATER ST N R
South Ferry BATTERY PARK 1·9
uptown
N
W — crosstown — E
S
downtown
© 1991 Tauranac, Ltd. All Rights Reserved.
Reprinted by permission of Tauranac, Ltd.
Express / Express-Local
Local
Skip-Stop
Transfer Between Routes
Call 718-330-1234 for Subway Information

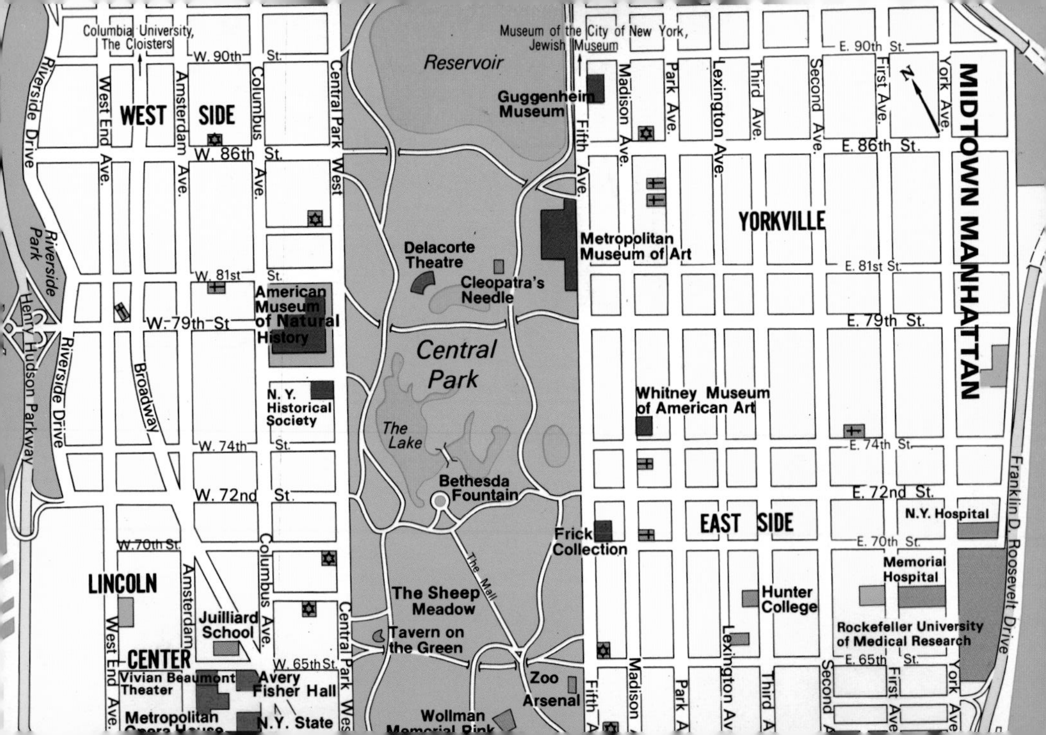
MIDTOWN MANHATTAN
N
Franklin D. Roosevelt Drive
York Ave.
First Ave.
Second Ave.
Third Ave.
Lexington Ave.
Park Ave.
Madison Ave.
Fifth Ave.
E. 90th St.
E. 86th St.
E. 81st St.
E. 79th St.
E. 74th St.
E. 72nd St.
E. 70th St.
E. 65th St.
YORKVILLE
EAST SIDE
N.Y. Hospital
Memorial Hospital
Rockefeller University of Medical Research
Hunter College
Whitney Museum of American Art
Metropolitan Museum of Art
Museum of the City of New York, Jewish Museum
Guggenheim Museum
Frick Collection
Reservoir
Cleopatra's Needle
Delacorte Theatre
Central Park
The Lake
Bethesda Fountain
The Mall
The Sheep Meadow
Tavern on the Green
Zoo
Arsenal
Wollman Memorial Rink
Central Park West
Columbus Ave.
Amsterdam Ave.
Broadway
West End Ave.
Riverside Drive
Riverside Park
Henry Hudson Parkway
W. 90th St.
W. 86th St.
W. 81st St.
W-79th-St
W. 74th St.
W. 72nd St.
W. 70th St.
W. 65th St.
WEST SIDE
American Museum of Natural History
N. Y. Historical Society
Juilliard School
Avery Fisher Hall
N.Y. State
Vivian Beaumont Theater
Metropolitan Opera House
LINCOLN CENTER
Columbia University, The Cloisters

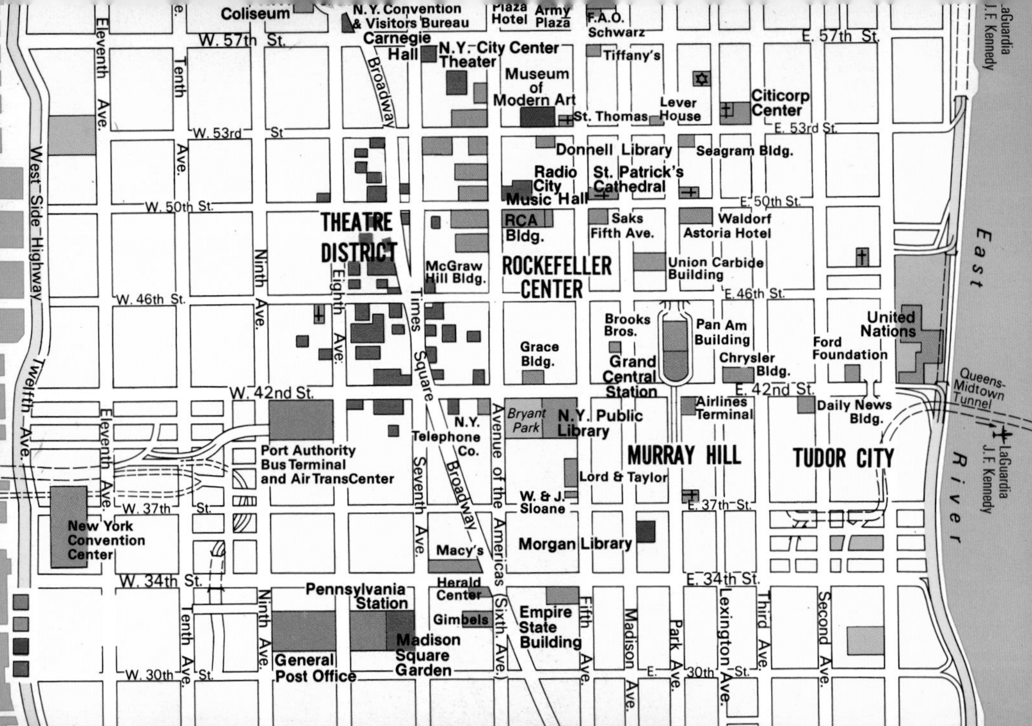

Coliseum
N.Y. Convention & Visitors Bureau
Plaza Hotel
Army Plaza
F.A.O. Schwarz
W. 57th St.
E. 57th St.
Carnegie Hall
N.Y. City Center Theater
Tiffany's
Museum of Modern Art
St. Thomas
Lever House
Citicorp Center
W. 53rd St
E. 53rd St.
Donnell Library
Seagram Bldg.
Radio City Music Hall
St. Patrick's Cathedral
W. 50th St.
E. 50th St.
THEATRE DISTRICT
RCA Bldg.
Saks Fifth Ave.
Waldorf Astoria Hotel
McGraw Hill Bldg.
ROCKEFELLER CENTER
Union Carbide Building
W. 46th St.
E. 46th St.
Brooks Bros.
Pan Am Building
Grace Bldg.
Grand Central Station
Chrysler Bldg.
Ford Foundation
United Nations
W. 42nd St.
E. 42nd St.
Bryant Park
N.Y. Public Library
Airlines Terminal
Daily News Bldg.
Queens-Midtown Tunnel
N.Y. Telephone Co.
Port Authority Bus Terminal and Air TransCenter
MURRAY HILL
TUDOR CITY
LaGuardia
J.F. Kennedy
Lord & Taylor
W. & J. Sloane
W. 37th St.
E. 37th St.
New York Convention Center
Morgan Library
Macy's
W. 34th St.
E. 34th St.
Herald Center
Pennsylvania Station
Gimbels
Empire State Building
Madison Square Garden
General Post Office
W. 30th St.
E. 30th St.
West Side Highway
Twelfth Ave.
Eleventh Ave.
Tenth Ave.
Ninth Ave.
Eighth Ave.
Times Square
Broadway
Seventh Ave.
Avenue of the Americas (Sixth. Ave.)
Fifth Ave.
Madison Ave.
Park Ave.
Lexington Ave.
Third Ave.
Second Ave.
East River

WALL STREET
City Hall, Chinatown
Murray Street
Park Place
Barclay Street
Vesey St.
Spruce St.
Beekman St.
Ann St.
Fulton St.
Park Row
Woolworth Building
St. Paul's Chapel
Broadway
Church St.
World Trade Center
Gold St.
Nassau St.
William St.
John St.
Platt St.
Maiden Lane
One Liberty Plaza
Liberty St.
Liberty Park
Cedar St.
Chase Manhattan Bank Bldg.
Pine St.
Federal Hall National Memorial
Wall Street
Trinity Church
Trinity Place
N.Y. Stock Exchange
Morgan Guaranty Trust Co.
Citibank
Exchange Pl.
Washington St.
Greenwich St.
Albany St.
Carlisle St.
Rector St.
West Street
West Side Highway
New Street
Broad St.
Beaver St.
Hanover Square
Pearl St.
Water St.
Front St.
Peck Slip
South Street Seaport
Franklin D. Roosevelt Drive
South Street
Elevated Highway
Old Slip
Jeannette Park
Stone St.
Fraunces Tavern
Bowling Green
U.S. Custom House
Whitehall Street
Bridge St.
State St.
Battery Pl.
Battery Park
Peter Minuit Pl.
New York Plaza
Port Authority
Castle Clinton
Brooklyn-Battery Tunnel
Promenade
Ferry Terminal
Statue of Liberty
Staten Island
N

INDEX

An asterisk (*) next to a page number indicates a map reference. Where there is more than one set of page references, the one in bold type refers to the main entry. For index to Practical Information, see page 99.

Alice Tully Hall 54
American Craft Museum 70
American Indian, Museum of **72**, 90
Apollo Theatre 61
Aquarium 90
AT&T InfoQuest Center 26
Atlantic Avenue **78**, 94
Avery Fisher Hall 54

Battery Park 38, 125*
~ City 43
Belvedere Castle **58**, 90
Bethesda Fountain and Terrace 58
Big Apple Circus 90
Boat trips 76
Botanical Garden Conservatory 78
Bowery 50
Bridges 22*, 77
Broadway 23, **27**, 85–6, 124–5*
Bronx Park 22*, 78
Brooklyn 8, 22*, **77–8**
~ Museum 64
Bryant Park 29

Carnegie Hall **27**, 86, 125*
Castle Clinton 38, 126*
Central Park 16, 17, **54–8**, 87, 90, 124*
Chase Manhattan Bank 39, 126*
Children's Museum of Manhattan 90
Chinatown **44**, 94
Chrysler Building **30**, 32–3, 125*
Churches
St. John the Divine 59
Riverside 59
St. Mark's in-the-Bowery 50
St. Patrick's Cathedral 11, 16, **26**, 125*
St. Peter's 30
Trinity 39, 126*
Cinemas 86–7
Circus 90
Citicorp Center 30, 125*
City Hall 39
City of New York, Museum **72**, 90, 124*
Cleopatra's Needle 58, 124*
Cloisters, The 70
Colonnade Row 50
Columbia University 21, **59**
Cooper-Hewitt Museum 70
Crystal Palace 16, 29

Delacorte Theater 58, 124*

East Village 49–50
Ellis Island 22*, 73–6
~ Immigration Museum 73
Empire State Building 18–9, **35–7**, 125*

Federal Hall Nat. Memorial 37, 126*
Fifth Avenue 24–6, 124–5*
Flatiron Building 17
42nd Street 27–30, 125*
Fraunces Tavern and Museum 15, **38**, 126*
Frick Collection 70–1, 124*

Grand Army Plaza 26, 125*
Grand Central Station 29, 125*
Grant's Tomb 59
Greenwich Village 17, **47–8**, 49*
Guggenheim Museum 71, 124*
Guiness World of Records 35

Harlem 17, 22*, **60–1**
Hayden Planetarium **63**, 90
Helicopter flights 76–7
Hicks Street 78
Holography, Museum of 72

IBM Gallery of Science and Art 72
Immigration, Museum of 73

Int. Center of Photography 71
Intrepid Sea-Air-Space Museum 72

Jewish quarter 47
Juilliard School 54, 124*

Laserium 63–4
Lincoln Center **52–4**, 86, 124*
Little Italy **47**, 94
Lower East Side 44–7

MacDougal Alley 48, 49*
Madison Square Garden **35–7**, 89, 125*
Metropolitan Museum of Art 64–6, 124*
Metropolitan Opera House 52–4, 124*
Mitzi Newhouse Theater 54
Modern Art, Museum of (MOMA) 66–8, 125*
Morris-Jumel Mansion 61
Moving Image, Museum 72
Museo del Barrio, El 61
Museums 62–72, 90. See also individual entries.
Music 86, 87

Natural History, Museum **62–4**, 90, 124*
NBC studios 23
New York Telephone Company Building 29
New-York Historical Society 72, 124*
New York State Theater 52, 124*
News Building 30

Old Custom House 38
Orchard Street 47

Pan Am Building 30, 125*
Performing Arts at Lincoln Center, Museum of 54, 86
Pierpont Morgan Library 72
Population 10
Public Library **29**, 31, 125*
~ at Lincoln Center 54, 86
Public Theater 50, 86

Radio City Music Hall 23–4, 125*
Rainbow Room, The 23
RCA Building (General Electric) 23, 125*
Ringling Brothers Barnum & Bailey Circus 90
Riverside Drive 59, 124*
Rockefeller Center 21–4, 125*

Schomburg Center for Research in Black Culture 61
Seagram Building 30, 125*
Shearith Israel Cemetery 44
SoHo 48–9
South Street Seaport Museum **43**, 72, 90, 94, 126*
Staten Island 13, 17, 22*
Statue of Liberty 16, 22*, **73–5**
Stock Exchange 37–8, 126*
Strawberry Fields 58
Studio Museum in Harlem 61

Theatre 85–6. See also individual entries.
Times Square 27, 125*
TriBeCa 49
Trump Tower 83

United Nations 17, **34**, 125*

Vietnam Veterans Memorial 38
Villard Houses 26
Vivian Beaumont Theater 54, 124*

W.R. Grace Building 29
Waldorf-Astoria 30, 125*
Wall Street 15, **37–43**, 126*
Washington Square 12, **47–8**, 49*
Whitney Museum of American Art 68–70
World Financial Center 43
World Trade Center 39–43, 126*

Zoos 58, 78, 90, 124*